The Kingdom Way

How the Kingdom of God Transforms our Lives, Churches, and Cities

Keith Wood

ISBN-13: 978-1505814569
ISBN-10: 1505814561

For King Jesus

Table of Contents

Acknowledgements

Many people over many years have contributed to the ideas in this book, a few knowingly, many more unknowingly. My exceptionally gracious wife, Patricia, has been a sounding board for these ideas since they first began to take shape. She has been a tireless support and companion and friend, and has yanked me back from many an edge.

My wonderful children, Devin, Alyssa, and Emma, have been patient with the seemingly endless hours spent on this project, and have cheered me on at many points.

Each of the authors I cite has had a huge influence on my thinking and spiritual growth and I am indebted to them for the hours and effort they poured into their works.

The faculty and staff of Montreat College and Moody Bible Institute contributed full courses of stone to the foundation of my spiritual life, and thus to the origins of this book. Late night talks with my mother cemented much of that foundation and gave the structure windows on reality.

Steve Brown taught me love of the Scriptures. Dennis Elster and Ray Lastra invested in me. CS Lewis taught me critical thinking. Charlie Sturges taught me spiritual warfare. Kevin Auman has been a fellow traveler through valleys and over peaks. Matt Auten inspired me with song. Brian Ingraham fueled me. Scott Burns affirmed me. Serenity Orr and Julie Vaughan provided invaluable editorial assistance. The little old ladies at church prayed for me, relentlessly, during my school years.

x

Introduction

There are well over one hundred references to the Kingdom of God or the Kingdom of Heaven in the New Testament. John the Baptist preached the Kingdom of God and called people to repentance and baptism. The Kingdom of God was a central theme of Jesus' teaching, occurring in the Sermon on the Mount, numerous parables, and in other teachings as well. And while the majority of passages mentioning the Kingdom of God occur in the Gospels, it is also referred to elsewhere in the New Testament. The apostle Philip preached the Kingdom of God in his ministry. Paul regularly taught the Kingdom of God and makes mention of it in six of his letters. James mentions the Kingdom of God, and in Revelation we see the summing up of all things in the Kingdom of God. The message of the Kingdom dominated the early church, yet we hear surprisingly little about it in churches today.

These days elders, pastors, churches and entire denominations struggle to find the balance between numerous seemingly competing emphases. Churches vary widely in their goals, some focusing on development of the individual, others on fostering community outreach. Striking the right balance seems difficult. In contrast, whatever it was that the New Testament church was doing succeeded in turning out highly effective people that spread the Gospel at an incredible rate. Could their message, practices, or priorities have been different than ours today?

Similarly, communal prayer in the New Testament was rich and fruitful, and appears to have been a normal activity of believers. Yet, how rare it is in churches today! Prayer meetings today are typically attended by only a few people and endure only a short while before disbanding, or worse, degenerating into weekly gossip sessions. Even pastors with a passion for prayer lose heart that they will ever see prayer flourish in their churches. What are we missing?

Again, in New Testament times, the Gospel obviously and radically changed people's lives. Fishermen boldly preached in the streets. Thousands at a time believed. Persecution drove people from Jerusalem and the Gospel spread like wildfire. Traveling evangelists had converts all over the known world, and the churches that were planted as a result of their work grew and sent out workers of their own. There was exponential growth the likes of which are rare today. The message preached in those days possessed a transformative quality that is often lacking today. Today many people profess to have "accepted Christ" but in comparatively few cases do their lives bear striking evidence of change. In many cases there is no evidence of change at all. Among believers who are endeavoring to contribute in their churches, many are weighed down by the burden of their responsibilities and have a difficult time rejoicing in their labors, having little sense that Christ works mightily within them.

Why is our experience today so different from that of New Testament believers? Could the missing ingredient be a comprehensive understanding of the Kingdom of God? It's possible.

What is the Kingdom of God, and how is it relevant to believers today? If you ask even mature believers this question, you are likely to get only vague answers. "It is Jesus as the head of the church." "God's sovereignty and salvation." "It is God at work in the world through Jesus." "It will be when we are all with Jesus after He returns." "God's rule and reign." These are typical responses. Yet John, Jesus, Philip, Paul, and others preached and ministered with the centrality of the Kingdom of God in mind and their world was changed.

Despite Bible education, a degree in Christian missions, and a considerable amount of personal study, it is only within the last decade that I think I have begun to understand the Kingdom of God correctly. I have spent many years involved in church, leading home Bible studies, teaching adult Sunday school classes, mentoring other men, and leading and participating in prayer. My conclusion after seeing what has worked and what has not is that we desperately need a comprehensive vision of the Kingdom of God that is clear, easily understood, and has a consistently central role in guiding our prayer and activities.

I have become convinced that the early church had such a vision of the Kingdom of God. Their understanding of the Kingdom affected their entire outlook, encompassing their study, preaching, devotions, prayer, and ministries. It helped shape everything they did, and equipped them so that God could work within and through them to transform people and their cities. They were successful because they lived by their vision of the Kingdom of God, and that allowed God to work through them with great power.

Can a powerful and compelling vision of the Kingdom of God be recovered? Can we live by a clear vision of the Kingdom as the early church did? The answer is a resounding YES!

In this book, I present a teaching that brings together numerous Scriptural themes under one roof, the Kingdom of God. We will see that there are clear concepts we can use to understand the Kingdom of God, and clear principles we can use to apply what we learn about it. Together these can have a great bearing on our message, devotional lives, churches, and even how we reach our cities for Christ. Far from merely theoretical, however, this teaching is immensely practical, with implications for many areas of life and ministry. Learning to live and minister by the Kingdom should drive a much-needed transformation in the way we relate to God, each other, and the world.

My prayer is that this book will help pastors, elders, church leaders, and maturing believers develop a clear and more complete vision of the Kingdom of God, and to consistently act and lead people according to that vision.

Chapter 1

A Kingdom Foundation

*He said to them, "Therefore every teacher of the law who
has been instructed about the kingdom of heaven is like
the owner of a house who brings out of his storeroom
new treasures as well as old. Matthew 13:52 NIV*

If we are going to accomplish God's purposes individually and
communally in such a way that the modern church has the power and
effectiveness of the first century church, we will need a thorough
understanding of the Kingdom of God and its relevance to all areas of
life and practice. In this chapter we will lay a foundation about the
Kingdom of God to which we will refer throughout the rest of the
book.

As we attempt to understand the Kingdom as it functions today, it is
worth looking at some historical context to establish our starting point.
At the time of Christ, contemporary conceptions of the Kingdom of
God drew heavily on prophecies in Daniel about an earthly kingdom
without end that would follow on the heels of other great kingdoms,
subjugating and surpassing them. They also recalled God's covenant
with David, that He would put a man from David's line on the throne
of Israel forever.

When Jesus came He talked about the Kingdom of God quite
differently, as something that was present, something that was near at
hand and current to the moment. He attributed healings and
deliverances to the Kingdom of God being at work. Jesus' view
seemed to be that the Kingdom of God was at hand because He
Himself was at hand. Likewise, when He sent out His disciples to
minister and preach, He told them to go proclaiming the Kingdom of
God with healing and miracles (c.f. Luke 9:2). Jesus had established

the pattern. By sending them out, He meant for the Kingdom of God to be at hand wherever they went as well. His idea of the Kingdom of God was for it to be testified with both preaching and power, whether He did that Himself or sent others to do so.

Jesus' strategy had to do with faith, repentance, forgiveness, and obedience rather than establishing a visible government. The Kingdom of God as Jesus taught and lived it was neither political nor military in nature. This fact was not lost on those around Him, and many of His followers fell away because they were not getting what they longed for. Hopes for an earthly, political kingdom were so high that after His resurrection, even His disciples were keen to know if He was at last going to establish the earthly kingdom they had been expecting.

> *Therefore, when they had come together, they asked Him, saying, "Lord, will You at this time restore the kingdom to Israel?" And He said to them, "It is not for you to know times or seasons which the Father has put in His own authority. But you shall receive power when the Holy Spirit has come upon you; and you shall be witnesses to Me in Jerusalem, and in all Judea and Samaria, and to the end of the earth."*
> **Acts 1:6-8[1]**

Rather than establishing an earthly Kingdom, Jesus directed them to continue the work of preaching and ministering the Kingdom as He had already shown them, calling people to repent and believe in the Gospel. As Jesus had said previously, His Kingdom was not of this world.

> *Jesus answered, "My kingdom is not of this world. If My kingdom were of this world, My servants would fight, so that I should not be delivered to the Jews; but now My kingdom is not from here."*
> **John 18:36**

It was a heavenly Kingdom, made up of those who would return to God and build their lives around His priorities, serving Him.

---

[1] Unless otherwise noted, all Bible quotations are from the New American Standard Bible.

Although many fell away, some stuck with Him and continued His work, preaching and ministering the Kingdom of God in the name of Jesus. Their concept of the Kingdom of God remained a driving force in their ministries. They saw the Kingdom of God as involving a plan originating from a King, complete with important goals and specific methods. They were empowered by the Holy Spirit to carry out that plan and did so with great effectiveness, winning whole cities and regions for Him and turning the Roman Empire upside down.

Since that time, many ideas have sprung up about the Kingdom of God, some highly spiritual in nature, others reviving an earthly component and looking for a temporal political order that will usher in peace and prosperity. Still others emphasize the coming millennial Kingdom of Jesus when He returns. A review of these many ideas is well beyond the scope of this book. Rather, our focus will be narrow, in the sense that we will seek to know the Kingdom of God only as it exists today, with Jesus in heaven and us on earth. This is the Kingdom as the disciples understood it in the first century, after the Holy Spirit had come on Pentecost.

Our goal is to understand the key points of the disciples' message and the source of their power and success. We will attempt to know God's will and ways as they did, as well as the irrepressible hope that spurred them on, for we desire a vision as powerful, potent and true as theirs. Fortunately, all of these have their roots in a proper conception of the Kingdom of God.

The Present Day Kingdom of God

In seeking to grasp the disciples' view of the Kingdom of God, people are commonly inclined to start with Jesus' teachings. After all, Jesus mentioned the Kingdom of God far more often than anyone else in the Bible. Yet that is not where we will begin. Since Jesus is now enthroned in heaven as the King of Kings and the head of His church, we will start there. We will take this chapter to get a clear picture of His present Kingdom from a heavenly perspective, and to do that we will start with Paul. In Colossians, Paul wrote:

> *Therefore if you have been raised up with Christ, keep seeking the things above, where Christ is, seated at the*

right hand of God. Set your mind on the things above, not
on the things that are on earth.
Colossians 3:1-2

Our first question is, "What are the 'things above'?" We want to know
what the things above are because, if a believer as effective as Paul
commands us to set our minds on those things, there must be a good
reason.

Most believers have at least a few ideas of what the Things Above
might be. Jesus, ascended to heaven, seated at the right hand of God, is
an obvious answer from the context. If we think a little longer, we can
add to our list. Revelation provides some material. There are angels
there. There are four living creatures and twenty-four elders. There are
prayers of the saints like incense in golden bowls. These are all good
answers to our question, but they don't get us much closer to
understanding the Kingdom of God. They also don't help us
understand why Paul commanded us to seek and dwell on them. Yet,
as we will see, the Things Above comprise the present day Kingdom
of our Lord Jesus and, as such, are central to our understanding of it.

Our goal in this chapter is to gain a clear and precise understanding of
the Things Above. To do this, we will follow a narrative of Jesus'
experiences that ends with His enthronement in heaven. We will also
see what else we can connect to that narrative, because it is not as
simple a story as we typically think. When we are done, we will be
able to look back at Paul's command about the Things Above and find
that we have obtained a concrete grasp of the Kingdom of God.

Our narrative starts in John 17. The context is the Last Supper. It is
Jesus' last evening before His crucifixion. After sharing the Passover
meal with His disciples and teaching them about the coming Holy
Spirit, He takes time to pray, and His prayer makes up most of John
17. Twice in this prayer He makes a particularly intriguing request of
the Father. Here are the passages:

I will remain in the world no longer, but they are still in the
world, and I am coming to you. Holy Father, protect them
by the power of your name—the name you gave me—so
that they may be one as we are one.
John 17:11

I do not ask on behalf of these alone, but for those also who believe in Me through their word; that they may all be one; even as You, Father, are in Me and I in You, that they also may be in Us, so that the world may believe that You sent Me.
John 17:20-21

In these passages Jesus prays that we would be one with Him and with each other just as He and the Father are one. This is a rather interesting request, to say the least, and one we will explore in greater detail as we move forward

To answer our first question about the Things Above we will have to answer a second question about these prayers. Our question now is, "How and when does this prayer get answered?" We must answer this question before we can answer our first question with clarity.

Many people feel that the answer to Jesus' prayers must come in the future when we are with Jesus, are without sin, and finally have perfect fellowship with Him. However from the last bit of verse twenty one we can see that, whatever the answer to this prayer is, it has something to do with providing credible evidence that Jesus came from God. Jesus says, "…so that the world may believe that You sent Me." Therefore, the answer must come before His return. In fact, it must come before we die and go to be with Him. So again we ask, "How and when does this prayer get answered?" The answer to this question lies in the narrative we will be following, the starting point of which is these prayer requests.

A Word About Miracles

However, let us take caution. We will be talking about a miracle. And not just any miracle, but a miracle that ranks among the most massive and astonishing miracles God has done. In doing so, we will also be looking at some of the most difficult and challenging passages in the Bible, the passages that discuss this miracle. Before we continue, a word about miracles is in order.

It's not hard to notice that when a miracle is recorded in the Bible, the specific details of how the miracle was accomplished are never given. Typically some information surrounding the miracle is provided, but nothing is said about the mechanics of the miracle itself. That's because miracles are intended to show us things about the character, purposes, or power of the miracle worker rather than the precise physical events that make up the actual miracle. Let's look at a few examples.

In the feeding of the five thousand, Jesus took a small amount of bread and fish and fed a huge crowd with it. However, we are told absolutely nothing about how the amount of bread and fish increased. He broke the bread, but how did it increase? We are not told for one reason: it is irrelevant. The point of the account is not to explain in scientific terms what occurred with pieces of fish and bread. The means by which Jesus manipulated matter to increase the food supply is not discussed at all. The miracle and the account of it demonstrate that Jesus was Lord over the entire situation, and was both willing and able to work for the sake of the hungry crowd. It reveals Him in His power and compassion. The point of the account is not to provide detailed information on *how* it was done, but to describe *what* was done so as to show who Jesus is.

Similarly, when Jesus turned water to wine, we are told next to nothing about what actually occurred inside the jars apart from the fact that what used to be water had become wine. We learn nothing about Jesus' insight into the nature of wine versus water, but we learn quite a bit about His appreciation for marriage as an event worth celebrating, and about His willingness and ability to reveal His nature through a miracle without being self-aggrandizing. Again the question of *how* is irrelevant. We are told *what* Jesus did, and are given an opportunity to learn something about Jesus from it.

All miracle accounts follow this pattern, and there is a good reason for this. If we were given increasingly detailed information on the mechanics of a given miracle, we would invariably come to some point where what ordinarily happens didn't happen, and some other extraordinary thing happened instead. In the wine jars, we would find that suddenly, astonishingly, there were fewer water molecules, and a myriad of other molecules had shown up instead, molecules that make up good wine. With the loaves and fishes, we would find that somehow, unexplainably, there was more and more. It hardly needs to be said, but miracles are miraculous. There is no escaping that with closer inspection.

In years past I did not understand this; my determination to put comprehension of the mechanics ahead of acceptance of the facts was a stumbling block to my understanding. I made little progress when I approached things that way. Seeing the events as miracles that fundamentally defied explanation changed all that.

We will be studying an amazing miracle. Therefore, it is important to focus not on *how* the miracle was done, but on *what* happened and what we learn about the miracle worker. The question we must have in mind is, "What was done?" not, "How was it done?" This bears emphasis because the passages we will be studying next are difficult ones. We may be used to approaching them with the *how* question in mind, when the point is to see them as describing a miracle. When we look only at *what* was done we are free to leave the mechanics of *how* to God. We are free to accept the miracle for what it is, a miracle, pure and simple.

A Journey With Jesus

We are starting our narrative with Jesus' prayer requests in John 17. We are asking, "How and when does this prayer get answered?" The first part of our narrative follows Jesus through ensuing events. We know what happened to Him soon after He prayed. A few hours later He was arrested, put through some phony trials, beaten savagely, and crucified. He died, was buried, and on the third day rose again from the grave. Forty days later, after having appeared to His disciples, He ascended into heaven and was seated at the right hand of God, where He prays for us.

Pictorially, we could say Jesus went through these five things:

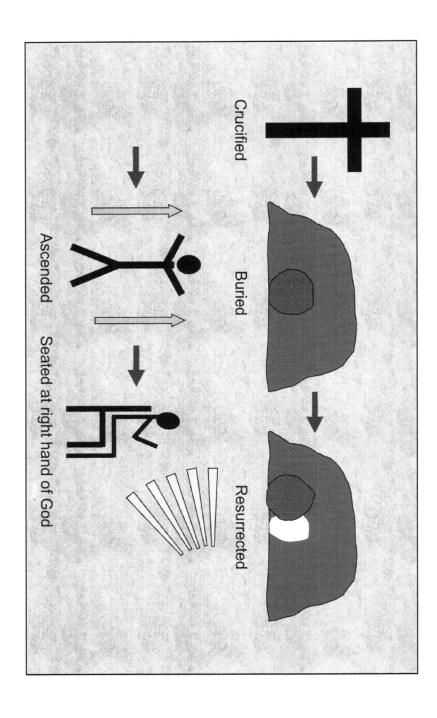

Recall in John 17 that Jesus asked the Father to make us one with Him and with each other, just as He is one with the Father. Soon after this prayer, He went through the five things we have just discussed. The second part of our narrative will connect the following passages directly with these events. Also, this is the miraculous part; if you have struggled with these passages, remember that you don't have to figure out *how* God did these miracles. Take the following passages at face value. Look at *what* happened, and put the *how* question aside.

Paul taught that he was crucified with Christ:

Paul, crucified with Christ

I have been crucified with Christ and I no longer live, but Christ lives in me. The life I live in the body, I live by faith in the Son of God, who loved me and gave himself for me.
Galatians 2:20

In fact, we all died with Christ:

All of us, crucified with Christ

What shall we say then? Are we to continue in sin so that grace may increase? May it never be! How shall we who died to sin still live in it? Or do you not know that all of us who have been baptized into Christ Jesus have been baptized into His death?
Romans 6:1-3[2]

---

[2] The baptism Paul refers to in these verses is not water baptism. Rather, Paul uses the word baptism the same way Jesus used it in Mark 10:38-39 and Luke 12:50, to refer to His death and burial. Jesus used this word a good while after having been baptized with water by John. Here Paul uses the term to describe the believer's union with Jesus in His death, which was an

We were buried with Him:

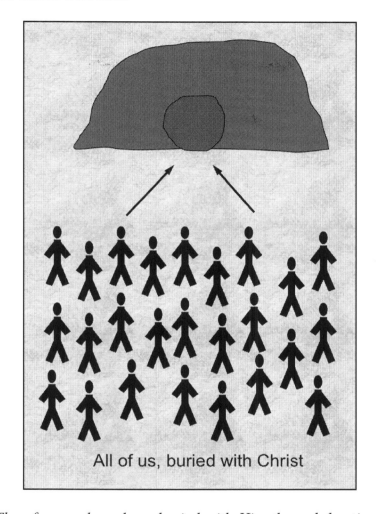

All of us, buried with Christ

Therefore we have been buried with Him through baptism into death, so that as Christ was raised from the dead through the glory of the Father, so we too might walk in newness of life. For if we have become united with Him in

immersion in the grave.

The confusion comes because we are used to thinking of baptism only as water baptism. However there is more than one usage of the term. One usage refers to the fact that we were joined to Jesus in death through our union with Him. Paul refers to this in Romans 6:3, and elsewhere. The other usage of the term denotes the sacrament that symbolizes our death and resurrection with Jesus by immersion in water.

the likeness of His death, certainly we shall also be in the likeness of His resurrection
Romans 6:4-5

We were also made alive with Jesus:

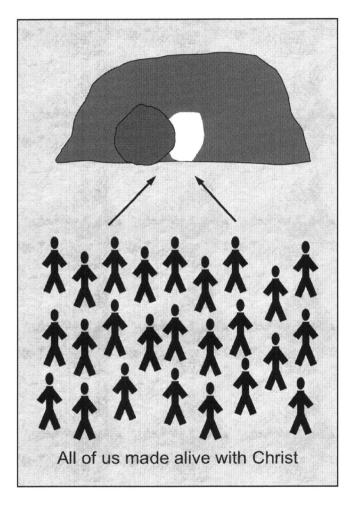

All of us made alive with Christ

...even when we were dead in our transgressions, [God] made us alive together with Christ (by grace you have been saved),
Ephesians 2:5

We were raised up with Him in His ascension:

All of us raised up with Christ

and raised us up with Him
Ephesians 2:6a

And we were seated with Him in the heavens, in Christ:

All of us, seated with, and in, Christ

and seated us with Him in the heavenly places in Christ Jesus
Ephesians 2:6b

Furthermore, concerning the Body of Christ, Paul wrote explicitly that we are one:

All of us made one with each other and Christ through the Holy Spirit and seated with Christ in the heavens

For even as the body is one and yet has many members, and all the members of the body, though they are many, are one body, so also is Christ. For by one Spirit we were all baptized into one body, whether Jews or Greeks, whether slaves or free, and we were all made to drink of one Spirit.
1 Corinthians 12:12-13

As we can see, the narrative of our union with Jesus perfectly parallels the narrative of His passion and exaltation. This is the miracle: We have been unified with Jesus and other believers through His death and resurrection. These things are true about us this moment.

This is also the answer to Jesus' prayer. We were made one with Him and each other, just as He asked. We can see that when Jesus died, somehow, through Him, we died too. When Jesus was buried later that day, we were buried too. When He was raised three days later, we were, too. And when He ascended and was seated in the heavenly places at the right hand of God, we were seated in the heavenly places, in Him, as well. The Holy Spirit was also given to believers, uniting us with each other and with Jesus. God completely answered Jesus' prayer within about a month and a half of His praying it. God made us one with each other and with His Son by joining us in our spirits through His Holy Spirit.

We will refer to this as the Present Day Kingdom of God[3], Kingdom of God, Heavenly Kingdom, or just Kingdom for short, and make reference to it using the image above. This understanding and depiction will form the foundation for much of what we discuss going forward.

The Present Day Kingdom of God

Why do I call this the Present Day Kingdom of God? There are several reasons. First, Jesus asked the Father for us, and now Jesus is enthroned as King over us through the relationships established for us in answer to His prayer. Kings inherit their kingdoms from those before them. In this case, Jesus inherited His Kingdom from the Father, Who had it before Him. We were given to Jesus as an inheritance, because Jesus asked the Father for us.

> *I pray that the eyes of your heart may be enlightened, so that you will know what is the hope of His calling, what are*

---

[3] The Millennial Kingdom, in which Jesus sits on a throne in Jerusalem, as well as subsequent expressions of the Kingdom, are discussed in many passages in the Bible. These eventualities will not figure prominently in our discussions. We want to understand the Kingdom as it exists right now, the Present Day Kingdom of God, because that was a main driver behind the success of the first century disciples, and it is our current context for Christian life and ministry.

the riches of the glory of His inheritance in the saints.
Ephesians 1:18

Second, we also receive *at the present time* a kingdom that cannot be shaken, which takes place through what Jesus accomplished.

> *Therefore, since we receive a kingdom which cannot be shaken, let us show gratitude, by which we may offer to God an acceptable service with reverence and awe;*
> **Hebrews 12:28**

Third, the disciples were known to acknowledge Jesus as King prior to the fulfillment of His earthly kingdom.

> *When they did not find them, they began dragging Jason and some brethren before the city authorities, shouting, "These men who have upset the world have come here also; and Jason has welcomed them, and they all act contrary to the decrees of Caesar, saying that there is another king, Jesus."*
> **Acts 17:6-7**

And as we will see throughout this book, Jesus' kingship is worked out through a proper understanding of His Kingdom as we've just defined it.

The Things Above

Remember that we went to John 17 and pursued this narrative to try to answer a different question, "What are the Things Above?" Let us return to Colossians and look back at Paul's command:

> *Therefore if you have been raised up with Christ, keep seeking the things above, where Christ is, seated at the right hand of God. Set your mind on the things above, not on the things that are on earth.*
> **Colossians 3:1-2**

Our spiritual union with each other and Jesus and our place with Him in heaven are, at least in part, what Paul refers to as the "things above." We can see some of these elements within the verses themselves. Paul mentions that we have been raised up with Christ, and that He is seated at the right hand of God. If we begin to inventory the various elements in our picture of the Heavenly Kingdom, we can see that you (if you are saved), other believers, Jesus, the Holy Spirit, the Father, and our unity with each other and Jesus through the Holy Spirit, are all Things Above. Now we have something concrete in mind when we think about the Things Above.

Since the Kingdom depicted in this way is a difficult concept to grasp, and is for many a different way of thinking of things, we want to be completely sure it is biblical. A good test is whether it helps explain other passages. If it makes things clearer, and is supported by the rest of Scripture, it passes an important test. Following are several passages from Colossians and elsewhere that either support our narrative about the Kingdom and how it got to be the way it is, or become more understandable through our depiction of the Kingdom.

> *For though I am absent from you in body, I am present with you in spirit and delight to see how disciplined you are and how firm your faith in Christ is.*
> **Colossians 2:5**

Here Paul refers to his spiritual union with the Colossian believers. He was far away when he wrote the letter, but because he knew the truth about believers' union with each other, he could truly say that he was present with them in spirit. He was not speaking metaphorically, but instead made reference to an invisible spiritual reality brought about by the Holy Spirit that was in keeping with what we have seen about the Kingdom of God. He knew the truth we have attempted to portray in our image of the Kingdom. Our concept of the Kingdom makes this verse clearer.

Here is another passage:

> *In him you were also circumcised with a circumcision not performed by human hands. Your whole self, ruled by the flesh, was put off when you were circumcised by Christ, having been buried with him in baptism, in which you were also raised with him through your faith in the working of God, who raised him from the dead.*
> **Colossians 2:11-12**

This passage clearly refers to our connectedness with Christ in His death and resurrection, and that this is God's doing. It fits perfectly into the narrative of our journey with Jesus. Paul also associates a great hope with this truth, that our sinful self was overcome as a result of the miraculous nature of our salvation. We will have more to say about that in later chapters. Again, this is consistent with our understanding of the Kingdom and how it came about.

And another:

> *When you were dead in your sins and in the uncircumcision of your flesh, God made you alive with Christ. He forgave us all our sins.*
> **Colossians 3:13**

This verse is difficult to understand if we focus on the *how* question - how God made us alive with Christ - but once we regard this as a miracle in answer to Jesus' prayer it becomes much easier to accept at face value. It fits the narrative perfectly.

And again:

> *Praise be to the God and Father of our Lord Jesus Christ! In his great mercy he has given us new birth into a living hope through the resurrection of Jesus Christ from the dead!*
> **1 Peter 1:3**

Peter also agrees with Paul in his understanding of our salvation. The resurrection of Jesus Christ was powerfully effective in providing us with a new life and hope. We know that this is the case because we were miraculously made one with Him in answer to His prayers. Our life ended and began anew through our journey with Jesus.

So we see that other Scriptures do support our interpretation of the Kingdom of God. The truth is that we could go on and on through additional passages that support this. However we are not merely attempting to create a tool for interpreting the Bible, although if we get that in the bargain that's good too! What we really want to learn is how to apply all these amazing truths so that others see that Jesus came from the Father as the Savior. That, after all, was central to His request.

The Message of the Church

As noted, the selection of verses above is weighted toward Colossians. That was intentional. Paul wrote the letter we call Colossians to a church he had never visited. The verses above and several others in Colossians contain statements that, without considerable prior understanding, would surely have been difficult to grasp. Paul clearly assumed the readers would know perfectly well what he meant by them because *he made no effort to explain them*. He simply threw these statements into the letter with the full expectation the readers would know what he meant. He assumed an in depth knowledge on the part of the Colossians believers, a level of understanding that would be rare in young churches today.

However, Paul does mention Epaphras, the missionary who established the church at Colossae. In view of the fact that someone else brought the Gospel there, it seems that the Kingdom of God *as we have understood it*, with all its component parts, was actually *the normal teaching of the early church*, so much so that Paul felt completely at ease in referring to these things throughout this letter. He knew the Kingdom of God, as we have described it, had been taught there. He could write the things he did because he knew the Colossian believers had learned enough to understand them. Apparently Paul and those associated with him wasted little time in conveying the more complex concepts of the Kingdom to the new churches of the time. This shows us how central the Kingdom as we have defined it was to the early church.

We see the same thing when we look at other references to the Kingdom of God outside the Gospels. The Kingdom of God was the apostles' subject matter. Here are several examples:

> *But when they believed Philip as he proclaimed the good news of the kingdom of God and the name of Jesus Christ, they were baptized, both men and women.*
> **Acts 8:12**

Paul entered the synagogue and spoke boldly there for three months, arguing persuasively about the kingdom of God.
Acts 19:8

They arranged to meet Paul on a certain day, and came in even larger numbers to the place where he was staying. He witnessed to them from morning till evening, explaining about the kingdom of God, and from the Law of Moses and from the Prophets he tried to persuade them about Jesus.
Acts 28:23

He proclaimed the kingdom of God and taught about the Lord Jesus Christ—with all boldness and without hindrance!
Acts 28:31

Jesus, who is called Justus, also sends greetings. These are the only Jews among my co-workers for the kingdom of God, and they have proved a comfort to me.
Colossians 4:11

Notice the one reference in which Paul argued persuasively about the Kingdom of God for three months. The Kingdom of God was the substance of the message the early church believed, preached, and lived by.

Jesus spoke about the Kingdom of God being at hand before the Things Above looked as they do now. He could do so because of His perfect relationship with His Father, the King. Paul could do so because Jesus had received His heavenly Kingship by that point, and had brought Paul into that Kingdom.

What is central to both periods is that the Kingdom of God was present on earth when God had people who would obey Him here. At present, those who obey God are the servants of Jesus, the present day King. We serve in the power that comes through the relationship we currently have with Him, the relationship that He established for us in the process of obtaining that kingship.

As we look back at Jesus' prayer, we should recall the reason He gave for praying it:

> *I do not ask on behalf of these alone, but for those also who believe in Me through their word; that they may all be one; even as You, Father, are in Me and I in You, that they also may be in Us, so that the world may believe that You sent Me.*
> **John 17:20-21**

Jesus prayed this prayer because He wanted the world to believe He was sent by God. He knew that if the Father granted His request, the church would then provide credible evidence that He came from the Father. In the days when Paul and Epaphras and others were circulating around the Roman Empire, the message they preached was transformative, exponentially fruitful, and firmly rooted in the Kingdom of God. The Kingdom was at hand because they were at hand, and that provided evidence that Jesus was the Savior.

I believe that the comparative lack of fruitfulness we see today can be tied to the fact that we have largely lost a coherent, precise, and detailed concept of the Present Day Kingdom of God. Once we recover right thinking and practices that are in keeping with the Kingdom of God, our fruitfulness will increase dramatically. If we desire to provide credible evidence to the world of Jesus as the Savior, then the Kingdom of God must become central to our message, lives, and methods. We must recover this.

In the following chapters, we will continue studying the Kingdom of God and look at how to apply Kingdom concepts to a number of areas. We will even add additional elements to our picture at some points. As we will see, the Kingdom is relevant to our individual lives, the message that we preach, our life as a community of believers, and our ministry to the cities in which we live. So "set your minds on the things above" and we'll forge ahead to see what this means for our lives and ministries.

Amy on the Rocks[4]

"OK. Check me," Amy said.

Joel stopped tying his rock shoes and looked up at her climbing harness. "Not too bad. Did you double back your buckle?"

She looked down. "Oops. Better do that, huh?" *Darn!* She thought. Why did she forget these things? She threaded the tail of the belt back through the buckle.

Joel was finished lacing his shoes and had started sorting the climbing gear she would need. "It's cool you're going to do this. I mean I know you're ready. It's just cool to be here with you leading this one for the first time. It's such a classic climb."

"I'm nervous."

"Don't be. You're ready for this. Just remember the stuff we talked about and you'll be fine. Besides, you've seen me do it."

"I know. You just make it look easy, that's all. I don't want to mess up," she said.

"You won't. Besides, who's watching?"

"Nobody. Well, you. That's enough, I guess," she answered.

"Shouldn't be worried about that. Here you go," he said, handing her the end of the rope.

She tied the knot into her harness and backed it with an overhand knot.

She saw Joel watching her, checking how she tied the knot. "Looks good," he said.

Standing back a couple steps, she surveyed the route above her. The sun had not yet hit the crest of the cliff above her. Though the air was cool, she felt sweat break out on her fingers as she looked up the face. It was granite, gray and light orange. Bright yellow lichens streaked the rock here and there. She closed her eyes, trying to remember all the things she needed to do. The contract, the route, all the advice she needed to recall. Opening her eyes, she said, "Ready."

---

[4] Each story in this book has a loose connection to the chapter following it.

"OK. Here's what you'll need for this one," Joel said. He handed her carabiners, runners, and various kinds of protection to place on the way up. Piece by piece she organized them on her belt, clipping them on.

"Remember what we talked about for this one?" he asked.

"Yeah. Up and to the right, following the crack. Straight up once I pass the little ledge. The crux is the vertical face. I'll want a cam for the flat crack and a runner ready to clip the bolt. Smooth sailing above that."

"Good. So what's next?"

"You hug me and wish me well!"

"Sure thing." They embraced. He felt so solid. She felt so...what was it? Fearful, but not of falling. What?

"You'll do great," he said, smiling. She held his gaze for a moment.

Now facing the rock, "OK. On belay." It was a contract between them. The point when the climbing formally began. A series of checks to let each other know they were one hundred percent tuned in to each other and nothing else.

"Belay is on," Joel said.

"Climbing," she replied.

"Climb on," he answered.

She stepped to the rock. Choosing handholds and footholds, she began moving up. This was the easy part. Stopping briefly, she set her first piece of protection in a crack and clipped the rope through the carabiner. She felt Joel let her have a bit of rope when she needed it for the clip, then snug it back to her. She felt secure in his belay, like he was sharing her mind as she moved.

Climbing again. Move, move, move. The rock felt good in her hands. The moves felt good flowing through her body. Chalk for her fingers. Stop. Place a piece, clip it. Move, move, chalk. Rhythm. At the little ledge now. Place a piece, clip it.

"I'm at the little ledge," she called down.

"You're great. Really smooth."

"Thanks," she said, more to herself. Concentrate. Straight ahead now. The next holds were slightly to the left. She added a runner to her last protection to smooth the rope's movement. Move, move. Steeper here, the toe of her shoe dragging on the rock as she pulled in close for a longer reach. A good foothold. Quickly placing a piece and clipping it. She was at the vertical face.

This was it. So far it had been fine. Just a couple challenging moves. She tried to rest but it was too steep to be a real resting place. She was holding herself to the rock. She looked up. The holds were smaller, the rock vertical. The horizontal crack was several feet above her. She checked her belt for the cam she would need there, changed its place on her belt to make it easier to grab.

"OK. I'm going."

"You'll be fine. Stay focused. You're doing great."

"Here I go."

Stepping up slightly she advanced a hand to a small handhold, just a finger ledge, really. She backed down, chalked up, tried to calm her left leg which was shaking up and down like a sewing machine. "Just go," she told herself. "You're on the rope. It's there for you. You can do this."

Back to the finger ledge. Moving, a foot, a hand, advancing. Focus, chalk, move. She scanned ahead for the next hold. The crack was just ahead. With another move, she was there. A nice handhold, good secure footholds on small sharp edges. She grabbed the cam and placed it beside her hand in the crack. It fit beautifully.

"Slack" she called to get a bit of free rope to clip it. Instantly it was there, the two feet she needed to pull up and clip it.

"Go, just go," she told herself. But her arms were getting pumped from pulling this vertical stretch. She moved, not wanting to lose momentum. Move up, grab the side hold on the thin flake to the left. Right hand to a pinch hold on a knob. Hardest part yet. Feet at the crack below her, room for one, no depth. Toeing a small depression with the other. Small step up to a better handhold. She could see the bolt she needed just ahead. Wide splay for a left foothold. Pulling in she lunged for the big edge above her. Got it!

Arms pumped, she grabbed a carabiner off her belt, clipped the rope to the bolt on her right. Her fingers were clumsy. Two hands to the ledge, a good, big hold. *Just a pull up,* she thought. She did it. Another big hold came in sight. Leg up, she was over!

Standing on the easy ledge she caught her breath. From below, "Woohoo! You smoked it!"

Breathing hard, she let one hand after the other hang down to rest. She wiped her brow, rubbing her sweaty hands on her shorts. It was warmer. The sun was hitting the rock now.

"That was intense," she called down between breaths. "Totally intense."

Joel's voice came back. "You did great. You had those moves cooked. Really great."

She looked but couldn't see him because of the ledge. "Yeah. Thanks. It felt really good. Give me a minute and I'll start up again."

Her arms were getting better and she had her breath now. A breeze cooled her. She looked out over the canyon, saw other climbers here and there. When did they arrive?

Shaking her head she called down, "OK. Climbing."

"Climb on," came the reply.

As soon as she moved she knew she'd messed up. The rope was dragging at the bolt. She hadn't added the runner to give it space and now it had to rub against the rock. No way to climb down to fix it. What should have been easy moves on big holds required hauling the rope up for every advance. "Stupid, stupid," she told herself. "Why did I do that?"

She worked her way up, setting protection, finishing at a large ledge with some cedars. Tying herself off, she called down. "Off belay."

"Belay off," came Joel's voice.

"I screwed up, Joel."

"What's wrong?"

"I left the runner off the bolt. There was a lot of rope drag. I won't be able to feel you while you climb, while I belay you."

Silence. The moment stung her.

"It'll be fine, Amy. You can top rope me. Just pull up all the rope when I tell you and you can throw it back down and top rope me. I can clean the gear just the same."

That would work. But it wasn't the flawless performance she had hoped for, and Joel's climb wouldn't be as fun. *Darn. Why did I do that?*

Joel again. "OK, I'm off the rope. You can pull it up now."

***

Joel came over the last edge smiling at her. "Good belay. Thanks." She offered him the webbing she was using as an anchor. Clipping in, he sat beside her. "Off belay," he said.

"Belay off." Contract closed.

"You did great. Your moves through the crux were just perfect. Like you'd done it before. It was cool watching you."

"Thanks." She was still kicking herself for messing up the runner. She started rearranging gear. She didn't feel like looking at him.

"What's wrong?" he asked.

"Nothing. Just screwed up that runner. Ruined the climb for you."

"You didn't ruin anything. You made it, which was the main point, and I made it too, thanks to you. You just forgot that one thing."

"I should have remembered."

"Next time you can." His hand went to her shoulder, pulling her closer for a side hug. She felt herself resisting. He was being gracious now, but she remembered that silent moment.

"Look," he said, "You can't expect to have it all perfect the first time. You can't. I don't expect that from you. You shouldn't expect it from yourself. You get better, that's all."

"Yeah, I guess." She sighed, leaning into him. They sat silent and looked over the canyon. It was quiet.

Chapter 2

The Kingdom and God's Word

*For the Word of God is living and active and sharper
than any two-edged sword, and piercing as far as the
division of soul and spirit, of both joints and marrow,
and able to judge the thoughts and intentions of the
heart. Hebrews 4:12*

How do we apply what we have learned so far? We might be tempted
to regard it merely as material for meditation, but that won't get us
very far when it comes to showing the world that Jesus came from the
Father as the Savior. Fortunately, there is a more systematic approach.
We will take guidance from a portion of the Lord's Prayer. Jesus
taught us...

> *"This, then, is how you should pray: 'Our Father in
> heaven, hallowed be your name, your kingdom come, your
> will be done on earth as it is in heaven...'"*
> **Matthew 6:9-10**

In this prayer we find two keys that we can use to draw applications
from our concept of the Kingdom of God. The first is that God desires
for His will to be done on earth as it is in heaven. We will view our
depiction of the Things Above as God's will *as it is in heaven.* We will
then develop applications by basing our earthly practices on a careful
consideration of the Things Above. The central assumption here is that
the Things Above are to serve as the model for much of what we do
here on earth. We will use this approach throughout the book and see
several ways in which the heavenly reality applies to our earthly lives.

The second key from the Lord's Prayer is that *it is a prayer*. Jesus tells
us to *ask God* for His will to be done. We know He *wants* His will to

be done, and we will see from applications we develop how we can have a role in that. But accomplishing His will here on earth is not merely a matter of our effort. There must be prayer as well. We must *ask Him* to bring about His will on earth. We can model everything we do on the things above, but without calling on God for His involvement, there won't be real fruit. We have already seen that miraculous involvement of God led to the Things Above. He raised us up and unified us in Christ. The central assumption here is that for His will to be done on earth, additional miraculous involvement is required, and it is obtained through prayer.

These two keys allow us to develop what I call the Kingdom Way. The Kingdom Way is to look at the Things Above, consider how they express God's will, and model applications on that, while emphasizing prayer for God to bring about the fruit of such obedience. The Kingdom Way links Things Above with our earthly lives through practical applications and prayer.

The Kingdom Way and God's Word

Now we are ready to see Kingdom Way in action. We will start with God's Word. Why there? It is the simplest area of the Kingdom of God to which we can apply the Kingdom Way approach, and it is foundational to everything else in this book.

How do we find God's Word in the heavenly Kingdom? We need to add it to our picture of the Things Above. The Scriptures tell us…

> *Forever, O Lord, Your word is settled in heaven.*
> **Psalm 119:89**

God's Word is settled in heaven, and is eternal like the other Things Above. Adding it to our picture of the heavenly Kingdom looks like this:

Just as Jesus says, the earth will pass away but His words will endure, so this shows that God's Word is eternal. It will persist forever as a settled matter.

What is our approach? First, we look carefully at the Things Above and see what we need to apply here on earth based on what we see in heaven. Second, we examine how prayer fits into bringing it about.

How is God's will done in heaven with regard to His Word? This verse teaches us that God's Word is *in heaven as a settled matter*. Biblical scenes of heavenly worship show God being exalted according to His glory as described elsewhere in the Scriptures. All present worship Him. The angels obey God. Jesus' status as the Savior of mankind is agreed by all present. In all these things, we see that what God Word says is taken as a settled matter in heaven.

Is that what we see when we look on earth? Is God's Word a settled matter here? To what extent is God's Word a settled matter to a Himalayan tribesman who has never heard God's Word in his own language? Is God's Word a settled matter to those who have heard the Gospel but never obeyed it? To those who have obeyed the summons to receive salvation through Jesus Christ but harbor areas of disobedience in their lives, is God's Word as much a settled matter as it ought to be? If a pastor preaches but uses quotes from men and examples from the world to the exclusion of God's Word, is he preaching as if God's Word is a settled matter? When people within our own community live however they like, scarcely knowing right from wrong, not even aware that God finds such sinful living deeply offensive, is God's Word, which defines right and wrong, a settled matter for such people?

Obviously, the answer to all these questions is no. And this points out something important. We can easily see that with regard to His Word, it is important for it to go forth into the world. The questions above begin to outline the many areas where the Word of God should be having an impact. His Word should be used to proclaim salvation to the lost. It should become an increasingly settled matter among those who believe. Believers should cling to His Word, using it diligently and carefully and frequently in all we do.

Where His Word is concerned, working toward these ends fits with God's desire for His will to be done on earth as in heaven. The Kingdom Way should affect the way we preach, the kind of works we engage in and support, and even the sorts of written materials we use in our devotions. Recognizing that most of the lost have no idea what God's Word defines as right and wrong should also prompt us to get His Word out in a way that makes such things clear. Similarly, people are unaware that God is a loving Father, and His Word speaks of that as well.

God gives His Word a central and eternal place in the heavens. Therefore, we also ought to give His Word a central and perpetual place in all we do. This is God's will, for His Word is potent and powerful to accomplish His ends. It should be a major part of our ministries...

> *All Scripture is inspired by God and profitable for teaching, for reproof, for correction, for training in righteousness.*
> **2 Timothy 3:16**

...and our devotional lives:

> *Like newborn babies, long for the pure milk of the word, so that by it you may grow in respect to salvation.*
> **1 Peter 2:2**

In fact, God's Word should be prominent in all areas of Christian endeavor, including:

- Preaching
- Teaching
- Exhortation
- Devotions
- Service
- Correction
- Training
- Worship
- Prayer
- Evangelism

When we give His Word this kind of emphasis, it will become an increasingly settled matter within and around us. What do I mean by a settled matter? God's Word is treated as a settled matter more when it is obeyed freely than when it is not. It is more a settled matter when it is acknowledged as true than when it is rejected. And it is more a settled matter in our hearts when it bears fruit than when it is disregarded.

However, this emphasis on using the Word of God does not mean we rigidly exclude our own words, or those of others. The point is to get the balance right, and we have examples of this in the Scriptures. When the walls of Jerusalem were rebuilt the people of the city assembled to hear the Word of God. Ezra read the Word of God aloud to them.

> *Also... the Levites, explained the law to the people while the people remained in their place. They read from the*

book, from the law of God, translating to give the sense so
that they understood the reading.
Nehemiah 8:7-8

The Levites explained the Word of God to the people, no doubt using their own words to convey the sense of the passages. Similarly, when Peter arose to preach to Jerusalem on the day of Pentecost, his numerous quotes from the Old Testament were woven into the theme of his own words to the people (Acts 2:14-36). There are many examples throughout Scripture that show God's Word being incorporated into preaching or writing alongside the words of those doing the preaching and writing.

But how much of God's Word should we use versus our own words? Is there a guideline to help us in balancing our message, some principal about the proportion of Scripture in our devotions and ministries? I believe so. Just as a rough calculation, consider that of the 7,958 verses in the New Testament, eight hundred twenty are quotes from the Old Testament. That is, taken as a whole, about one tenth of the verses in the New Testament are quotations of Old Testament verses. A tithe! Through the miraculous work of inspiration, God caused the proportion of quoted Scripture to constitute about a tithe of all that the New Testament authors wrote.

Seen another way, the writers were so reliant on the Scriptures that at any given instant, there was about a ten percent likelihood they would quote the Old Testament as they wrote. What's more, an examination of the context surrounding these quotes shows that they were quite important to the messages the writers were endeavoring to convey. The writers were not just giving a token nod to the Old Testament then pressing on with their own thoughts. They saw the Scriptures as crucial to the arguments they were making. The Scriptures were central to their communication of truth, and they treated them as a settled matter.

This is a good guideline for us as well. We can examine our own preaching, teaching, devotional materials, worship song lyrics, and the like to see how well they measure up to this standard. I believe if we move toward greater reliance upon Scripture, we will honor God by showing we align with His desire for His Word to become a settled matter here. When we purposely use God's Word to accomplish His ends, it *will* have an effect on us, those to whom we minister, and the lost in our communities. It is His Word, living and active.

Prayer and God's Word

Of course, that is not all the Kingdom Way has to show us. It only covers how we proceed once we have recognized that God's Word going forth is His will being done on earth as in heaven. The Kingdom Way approach has two parts: modeling our strategies and tactics on the things above, which we've just discussed; and praying for God's intervention so that His miraculous involvement will also take place. We are to do God's will as we see it in heaven, *and* soak that effort in prayer for Him to move and bring the fruit.

This points out a need in us of which we might be unaware. God desires for us to be dependent on Him in all areas of our lives and ministries. Those of us who have received salvation through Jesus Christ are aware that we are dependent on Jesus for our standing and relationship with God. By instructing us to call upon Him for His will to be done, God wants us to recognize that, even in the execution of our responsibilities, we must depend on His involvement if there is to be any real fruit.

So, if it is preaching the Gospel, we must use God's Word to tell of the grace that He offers through Christ, and also call people to repentance by making clear what He considers to be sin. This is part of God's Word going forth, and we see John the Baptist doing this when he answers questions from the crowd in Luke 3:10-14. John spells it out clearly for them so that it will become a settled matter. But alongside all this we must also call upon God in prayer when we prepare and use His Word, so that it will bear fruit and become the settled matter it is meant to be. We must pray for the hearers, that God's Spirit will move through His Word with good effect. Only when it begins to settle in the hearts of people will God's Word bring forth the fruit He desires.

If it is teaching, we must fill our teaching with the Word of God, and we must pray for God to move by His Spirit through His Word as it goes forth in our teaching. But this is not just a single prayer said before we teach. It includes prayer that the message will be in keeping with His will and Word, prayer that we will be spiritually prepared as the messengers, and prayer for the people that will hear the message.

Prayer for all of these is important for God's will to be done. If we neglect prayer in any of these, the result will be less than it could be, even if we have used God's Word.

When it comes to our personal devotions, God's Word should be central. Yet, many believers use devotional materials that scarcely rely on the Word of God. They are filled with the thoughts and meditations of men. In contrast, God wants His Word to go forth in us and become an increasingly settled matter. It is largely through His Word that He speaks to us and instructs us. His Word is the final guide for faith and practice. But should we not also pray for His Word to go forth within us? Some things are hard to accept and obey. By praying for His Word to go forth and become an increasingly settled matter we gain His power and involvement in our own devotional lives. We invite Him to be involved in our growth rather than trying to bring it about merely through our devotion to His Word.

Neglect of God's Word in our devotions reveals disbelief that His Word going forth in us has power to change us. It shows that we believe that we can pick whatever we want as food for our souls, even well meant but Scriptureless words of other believers, and it will be good enough. But consider how the New Testament writers showed such high regard for God's Word, using it so frequently. Were they not wise? Let us follow their example and rely on God's Word in our devotions. God's Word is in a different category than the words of men. It is powerful to work within us in ways that the words of men are not.

> *For the Word of God is living and active and sharper than any two-edged sword, and piercing as far as the division of soul and spirit, of both joints and marrow, and able to judge the thoughts and intentions of the heart.*
> **Hebrews 4:12**

Conversely, if we read His Word, but do so prayerlessly, we reveal a heart that believes the things of His Word can be correctly understood through our human minds alone. We demonstrate that we believe we do not need God for His miraculous intervention and involvement in making His Word go forth within us. But God's Word says:

*The heart is more deceitful than all else and is desperately
sick; who can understand it?*
Jeremiah 17:9

We need to be in God's Word, taking God's Word into us, but we also
need to be in prayer all the while, that His Word will sink down into us
and bring forth fruit. We must defer to God's Word as the measure of
our lives, and through prayer, call upon Him that He will bring
conviction of sin wherever needed. The Kingdom Way shows us that
His Word should go forth within us, which happens by using it and
welcoming it, and praying for it to have its intended effect. Just as
John says:

> *I have written to you, young men, because you are strong,
> and the Word of God abides in you.*
> **1 John 2:14b**

In worship, we should be reading His Word, singing His Word, and of
course obeying His Word. It is worth asking ourselves why we sing so
many songs that are words of men when there are so many songs taken
straight from Scripture. Using God's Word in public worship pleases
God because by it we demonstrate that He and His thoughts are
important to us, and it also becomes a means by which those present
have the Word go forth to them. But again, our prayers that God will
accompany our worshipful use of His Word are critical to its
fruitfulness.

In our prayers, both public and private, we should incorporate His
Word, praying it back to Him. We prove that His Word is precious to
us when we use it in our prayers.

Preaching that omits His living and active Word will be ineffective
because it will lack the potency of His Word. Preaching without prayer
will be ineffective because the Holy Spirit will not carry forth the
Word of God to the hearts of the hearers and bring forth fruit. Both are
needed, the Word and much prayer. Neglect of either will leave us
talking into the wind.

If we carefully examine our lives and ministries we will find there are
many areas in which we can incorporate God's Word, if we are only
purposeful to do so.

Conclusion

God's Word exists in the heavenly Kingdom as a settled matter. The Kingdom Way shows us that God's Word should become an increasingly settled matter on earth, and that prayer and broad use of His Word are required for this to take place. God's Word, being powerful, is meant to be the backbone of our teaching, preaching, and devotions. It is meant to have a central place in all we do, and to be empowered by the Holy Spirit in answer to our prayers. In this way the message will be God's, and will have power. When this takes place, Jesus will become more widely known as the Savior sent by God, just as He prayed.

Challenges

Study occurrences of the words earth and heaven together throughout the Bible. How strong a theme is God's will being done on earth as in heaven? What additional areas besides God's Word can you identify?

Do you set your mind on the things above? Memorize the Scriptures that contributed to our picture of the Things Above. Spend periodic purposeful time meditating on them. Pray for understanding of their truth without worrying about how God brought them about.

Examine your devotional life. Do you use God's Word, or mainly other materials? Increase your use of God's Word. Pray that in your use of God's Word He would move to bring forth fruit. Identify any areas of your life in which you are resisting letting God's Word become a settled matter. Repent and prayerfully surrender to God in these areas.

If you have a ministry or area of service, identify three ways in which you can increase your use of God's Word. Act on those. Pray accordingly for each one that God will move through your use of His Word to bring forth fruit.

If you are involved in leading public worship, identify ways in which you can increase the proportion of God's Word. Are you and your worship teammates praying for God's Word to be a powerful part of the worship? If not, dedicate purposeful time to praying for this, and guard the time spent in prayer as a critical component of your preparation. Discuss whether your primary purpose is for the music to sound great or for the Holy Spirit to have His way. Set enough time aside for adequate prayer *and* adequate practice so the Holy Spirit gets His way, *and* it sounds great! Examine Scriptural scenes in heaven and observe to what extent the words of praise there are spoken versus sung. Model how you use the Word on that balance.

If you preach, teach, correct, exhort or train others, do so using God's Word. Set aside purposeful times of prayer to discern the passages God would like you to use. Pray also that His Word would go forth with His power to accomplish His purposes.

To what extent do you use God's Word in prayer? Increase this. Identify Scriptures that define God's desires and pray for His will to come about using the words themselves. Build up a set of such verses that apply at all scales, from your self, to your church, to your city and beyond.

Take the 1 Timothy 4:13 Challenge! Paul wrote:

> *Until I come, give attention to the public reading of Scripture, to exhortation and teaching.*

With some friends, go to a public place such as city hall, a public park, or a street corner, and read Scripture aloud. While one reads, have the others pray for God's will to be done and for His Word to go forth with power and become a settled matter in your city. Be prepared for interesting opportunities to arise from obeying this command. Pray beforehand about which Scriptures God would have you read. Do this regularly as part of your effort to reach your city.

Highway Miles

Joel leaned forward to turn down the car stereo a bit, not taking his eyes off the road. "He was on the way home from work. It happened a block from our house. Drunk driver came out of the side street and T-boned him in the driver's side."

"Oh, man, Joel. I'm so sorry."

"They said it was quick."

Amy hardly knew how to reply. It was too horrible. His dad, killed so senselessly. What do you say to that?

"You've never talked about it," she ventured.

"I'm just getting to where I can, I guess."

She waited. His brows had that furrowed look. His lower lip, tight, made the hairs of his beard stick out straight. He wasn't done. They slowly passed a semi with two trailers. Joel was motionless except for small corrections of the wheel.

"I miss him."

Still, the brows. An off ramp came and went. Another mile.

"I miss the good times we had, fishing, snowmobiling."

She wondered how he could say it without crying.

"He was always good to me. Never hard on me."

He was going somewhere with this. A motorcycle passed them. Nebraska countryside rolled by. More miles.

"I don't know," he said, shaking his head.

Amy looked over. Still had that focused look. "Don't know what?" She was guessing. This was new territory.

He turned and looked full in her face. His eyes were, what? Fiery? Teary? "I don't know why I'm mad at him."

"Who?"

"My Dad."

Eyes back on the road, head forward, brows down, lips straight. His neck looked stiff. *Best leave that alone,* she thought. *Give him time.*

***

"Want something to drink?" she said. An hour had passed. She had checked her email three times, written two, read a blog she followed. She'd surfed the web, found nothing of interest in the news, checked the weather – sunny and upper eighties for days ahead – and watched miles go by.

"Sure. What do we have left?" He seemed a bit more relaxed.

Whew! she thought. Digging around behind her, "There's water, some apple juice. One frappe, not so cold now." she said, relieved to have broken the silence.

"I'll have juice."

She opened it and handed it over.

"Thanks," he said. "Look, I'm sorry to drop that on you like that and leave you hanging. I just needed some time to think about it some more. It seems like I can only just start to see him clearly now and it's a lot to get through."

"That's OK. I don't mind waiting. I figure it's big stuff." She rubbed his shoulder briefly. "Any progress?"

"I think so," he said. "I think I'm mad at him because he was more of a pal than a father. I mean we did all these fun things. He loved to have fun and we did all these great things. Every weekend we were off doing something. Water skiing, hunting. It was never a dull moment." He trailed off.

"What's wrong with that?" she asked.

"It's just that that's all there was. I feel like I was starving for something more serious, that never came, you know?"

"Like what?"

"Like, maybe, how you live your life so you don't screw up."

"What do you mean?"

"When I left for school, I just got in one kind of trouble after another. Partying with the guys. In jail for public drunkenness. Never even made grades I could wreck. All that stuff. Bombed out. We've talked about it. I was just such a mess. Like I had no sense at all." He paused. "Shouldn't he have given me a little guidance? I mean, wasn't that his job or something? Anyway, that's what it seems like right now. That's why I'm angry at him. Maybe I'm wrong. I don't know."

"That's how you see it, though, so that's fine. You'll sort it out. You've got to know this is part of processing, so it's probably healthy. Weird thing is…He sounds like the exact opposite of my Dad. You've heard me talk about him before. Always on me about everything I didn't do right. I've spent plenty of time mad at him, believe me."

"Yeah, I remember that. I guess that is pretty weird, how they're opposites, and all. Never thought of that."

Chapter 3

The God of the Gospel

Sing praises to God, sing praises;
Sing praises to our King, sing praises.
For God is the King of all the earth;
Sing to him a psalm of praise.
Psalm 47:6-7

In the last chapter, we saw that the Word of God is to be central to our teaching and preaching, lives and ministries. We also saw that God wants His Word to go forth with power through our prayers and efforts, and to become an increasingly settled matter everywhere. In this chapter we will concern ourselves with how someone gets added to the picture below. How, from an earthly standpoint, do they come to have a place in this assembly?

We already know that it is through the cross, grave, resurrection and exaltation of Jesus that anyone comes into this heavenly assembly. From an earthly perspective, we also know that it doesn't happen in a vacuum, without the person coming to grips with a message of great importance. But what is that message? If we are going to preach and minister using the Word, we ought to have a clear idea what the Gospel message is, and as we shall see, the Things Above have some bearing on the answer.

The Message in Jesus' Day

In order to understand the Kingdom Way here, we will need to look at some Scripture passages and see what we can learn from the message and interactions of Jesus and John the Baptist. Early in the Gospels we see John the Baptist preaching a message of repentance.

> *John the Baptist appeared in the wilderness preaching a baptism of repentance for the forgiveness of sins.*
> **Mark 1:4**

Elsewhere, we see John being specific about what repentance would mean for various people.

> *And the crowds were questioning him, saying, "Then what shall we do?" And he would answer and say to them, "The man who has two tunics is to share with him who has none; and he who has food is to do likewise." And some tax collectors also came to be baptized, and they said to him, "Teacher, what shall we do?" And he said to them, "Collect no more than what you have been ordered to." Some soldiers were questioning him, saying, "And what about us, what shall we do?" And he said to them, "Do not take money from anyone by force, or accuse anyone falsely, and be content with your wages."*
> **Luke 3:10-14**

In context, there were many people being baptized by John. His good news connected repentance with salvation, with baptism as the outward sign of obedience.

*And he came into all the district around the Jordan,
preaching a baptism of repentance for the forgiveness of
sins.*
Luke 3:3

When Jesus came along, He also began His ministry with a call to
repentance.

*From that time Jesus began to preach and say, "Repent, for
the kingdom of heaven is at hand."*
Matthew 4:17

His ministry involved baptism as well.

*Therefore when the Lord knew that the Pharisees had
heard that Jesus was making and baptizing more disciples
than John (although Jesus Himself was not baptizing, but
His disciples were), He left Judea and went away again
into Galilee.*
John 4:1-3

And like John, Jesus' message linked repentance and forgiveness.

*...and that repentance for forgiveness of sins would be
proclaimed in His name to all the nations, beginning from
Jerusalem.*
Luke 24:47

There was a great deal of similarity between Jesus' message and
John's. We could stop here and assume that we had discovered the
Gospel message as one of repentance for forgiveness, but there is
actually a good deal more going on. Grace is a prevailing theme
throughout the New Testament, and we need to see how that fits in.
Most of us have grown up with a message that centers on grace
without much reference to repentance. Passages such as this...

*For by grace you have been saved through faith; and that
not of yourselves, it is the gift of God; not as a result of
works, so that no one may boast.*
Ephesians 2:9-10

…seem to characterize the message we preach and hear far more often. It doesn't mention repentance at all, and many of us are uneasy throwing repentance into the mix with grace because that smacks of works, precisely what the verse above indicates salvation is *not* based on.

As it turns out, we actually see a variety of messages recorded in Scripture. The two extremes appear to be…

- A call to repentance from sin.
- A call to receive grace.

There are also some statements that seem to lie in the middle. To see how these reconcile in the Kingdom context, we will look at some of the messages we see in Scripture, and map them out on this line.

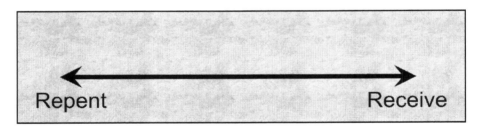

As we go through these, please remember that these are just my own highly subjective impressions from taking the wording at face value and out of context. By treating the verses this way, I do not mean to play fast and loose with the Scriptures. I merely intend to take statements as they appear, and gauge their content accordingly. These are not meant to be definitive interpretations, just a quick glance that will serve the purpose at hand and make a point. So bear with me. When we get through several passages, we'll stop and see if we've learned anything. Here's the first verse:

> *From that time on Jesus began to preach, "Repent, for the*
> *kingdom of heaven has come near."*
> **Matthew 4:17**

This verse only talks about repentance. Matthew does not even call this message the Gospel. Taken at face value there is no obvious good news within this verse. It is solid repentance. I plot it with the vertical arrow here:

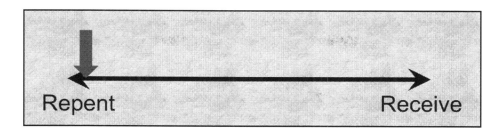

Here is the next verse.

> *Now after John had been taken into custody, Jesus came into Galilee, preaching the Gospel of God, and saying, "The time is fulfilled, and the Kingdom of God is at hand; repent and believe in the Gospel."*
> **Mark 1:14-15**

This verse starts to show that there is some good news involved. Jesus is preaching "the Gospel of God," so there is good news in the message somewhere, although it is not spelled out for us. There is also mention of believing in the Gospel, which hints at faith. Nonetheless it is heavy on repentance and vague about the rest, so I'll plot this one as shown. Again, these are quick subjective interpretations. It is not critical exactly where we plot these, and that should become clear when we are done.

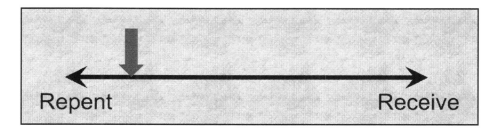

Here is another.

> *John the Baptist appeared in the wilderness preaching a baptism of repentance for the forgiveness of sins.*
> **Mark 1:4**

This verse is still long on repentance, but indicates there is forgiveness as well, not merely the hard work of repenting. It would naturally require some faith to believe in the promised gift of forgiveness. That is the receiving part. This verse portrays a nearly equal mix of repenting and receiving. I plot it here:

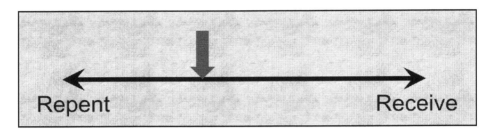

And another, this time recounting Philip's ministry.

> *But when they believed Philip as he preached the good*
> *news of the Kingdom of God and the name of Jesus Christ,*
> *they were baptized, both men and women.*
> **Acts 8:12**

In our quick tour through these passages, this verse turns a corner. There is no mention of repentance. The message is called the "good news of the Kingdom," which was believed by the people. Their response clearly involved faith. However, mention of the Kingdom of God introduces, perhaps, a bit of weightiness to it. There is a king, apparently. Taking this verse as a stand-alone summary of the message, one might be left to wonder just what significance this king might have. There is certainly something worth receiving, but might there also be something else, something demanding? It is not clear from just this verse. I see this one here:

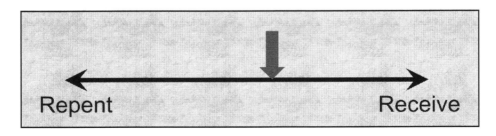

One more, then we'll stop and discuss what we've seen so far.

For God so loved the world that he gave his one and only Son, that whoever believes in him shall not perish but have eternal life.
John 3:16

There is no mention of repentance, no potentially dangerous king. Pure grace. This one plots cleanly at the Receive end.

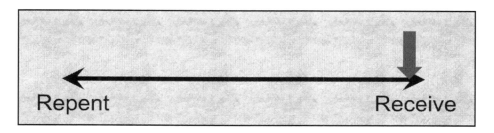

And here is how they all plot relative to each other:

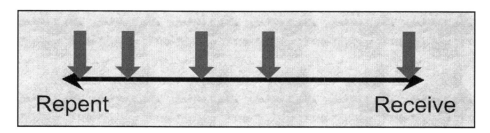

There is obviously a broad spectrum both in the message that was presented to people, and how the authors characterized that message in their writings when generalizing their accounts. We could look at more of these and plot them on the line, but we would merely end up filling in the distribution more completely. Sometimes the message is heavy on repentance. At other times it is heavy on receiving. In still other cases, it looks like something in the middle. Some people get one message, others get the opposite message. How do we make sense of this?

The God of the Gospel

Recall that our approach to the Kingdom is to model our lives and ministries on the Things Above. We get this approach from the Lord's Prayer, in which we are told to pray that God's "will be done on earth as it is in heaven." Let's quickly look back at this prayer, because within it we find the way to understand what we've seen so far. This bit is as much as we need:

> *Our Father in heaven, hallowed be your name. Your kingdom come…*
> **Matthew 6:9-10a**

Within this prayer Jesus portrays God as both King and Father. And herein lies our answer. We see different messages because sometimes people are being asked to respond to God as a king, One Who expects obedience. That is the message of repentance. At other times they are shown that God is fatherly and compassionate. That is the message of grace that must be received. The two end points on our line, repent and receive, are the two responses that are required of people who come to know God as both King and Father, as He portrays Himself. When we know Him and portray Him this way, His will is being done on earth as in heaven, for this is how He is known in heaven. Numerous verses, especially in the Sermon on the Mount, characterize God as our *heavenly* Father. Similarly, if there is a Kingdom of God, then there is a King.

God's identity is one of the Things Above. When we present the true Gospel, we must present God as He says He is, and that includes portraying Him as King and Father. This is the Kingdom Way, and it is how Jesus portrayed God.

The points along the middle of the line are there because the Gospel writers were summarizing what was being said. They were not being definitive, presumably because they were largely writing to people that had already come to know God as both King and Father.

Now, to be sure, there is more to the Gospel message than just King and Father. There are also important points about sin, our broken relationship with God, the impossibility of restoring that relationship on our own, what Jesus did to solve that problem, and the nature of our response, which is to have faith in Jesus apart from any reliance on our own works. These are critical elements of the Gospel. But to the uninformed, which includes most unsaved people and many in the church, who God is and how He presents Himself in the Scriptures are by no means clear. Therefore, we do people a disservice if we leave out one or other aspect of God as He wishes to be known.

We've also seen that some people got one message and others got a quite different message. Let's look more closely at a few passages and try to discern why the message changed based on the audience. Consider the woman caught in adultery, recounted in John 8:3-11. This woman was on the verge of being stoned to death, but through Jesus' intervention, she was spared. He challenged those around to throw the first stone if they were free of sin. Before long nobody was left accusing her. Whatever Jesus wrote in the dirt appeared to shame them, and they left one by one. Finally, with no accusers left, Jesus showed her ultimate grace.

> *Straightening up, Jesus said to her, "Woman, where are they? Did no one condemn you?" She said, "No one, Lord." And Jesus said, "I do not condemn you, either."*
> **John 8:10-11a**

Sweet words of life these were to her! But then He added this bit.

> *"Go. From now on sin no more."*
> **John 8:11b**

In essence, His command to her was to repent. Why? Because she had just received immense grace. Believing and receiving grace was not hard for her at this point. She had just experienced it in the form of a marvelous reprieve from certain death; grace rather than condemnation from Jesus. Before her eyes the man of miracles, a powerful prophet of God, had procured redemption for her. Grace was not at all difficult for her to believe at that moment. The challenge for her was to repent. Jesus discerned that beyond receiving grace she still needed to come to grips with God as a King, to whom she owed repentance and obedience.

We see the opposite in the case of the sinful woman in the Pharisee's house in Luke 7:36-50. This woman approached Jesus weeping over her sins. Filled with grief, she shed her tears on His feet, wiping them away with her hair. She went on worshiping Him, kissing His feet and anointing them with perfume. There is scarcely a more beautiful depiction of grief over sin anywhere in the Scriptures. What is Jesus' response to her?

> *Then He said to her, "Your sins have been forgiven....Your faith has saved you; go in peace."*
> **Luke 7:48, 50b**

Such reassurance! She came to the room fully aware of her sinfulness, apparently having repented. The burning doubt in her mind was whether she could be forgiven by God. She was in wrenching agony over this issue, to the point of desperate measures – to enter a Pharisee's house and utterly humiliate herself before everyone. Her only desire was to fall broken before Jesus in worship in hope of receiving some grace from Him. And grace she was given, total and free. Repentance was not her issue. She needed nothing other than to receive that which she knew she did not deserve, the forgiveness of her sins. She had hope enough to come to Jesus for it, but no certainty that she would obtain it. Her challenge was to believe that God could extend Fatherly kindness to her through Jesus.

We see the same dynamics in play in other passages. When the man was healed at the Pool of Bethesda, Jesus later reminded him to repent.

> *"Behold, you have become well; do not sin anymore, so that nothing worse happens to you."*
> **John 5:14b.**

Conversely, Jesus called Matthew (Matthew 9:9-10) to leave his tax collecting as a costly act of repentance. When Matthew obeyed, he received the grace of a relationship with Jesus. Yet again, Jesus shows grace to Zacchaeus (Luke 19:1-10) by choosing to stay with him, and Zacchaeus' response was repentance.

What does this say about our message? These days in most churches there is a strong emphasis on grace and much less emphasis on repentance. But by understating the need for repentance, we are failing to portray God as a King to whom obedience is due. The result of this is churches full of people who see no pressing need to live holy and blameless lives. God is not honored by this misrepresentation, and it is a failure to live the Kingdom Way that leads to it.

In contrast, there are churches in which repentance is urged in such strong terms that there is no grace at all, only judgment and fear. This leads to legalism. People get weighed down with guilt because God is not also portrayed as a Father full of grace, who receives sinners despite their sins. This is also a failure to live by the Kingdom.

The God of heaven desires to be known as both King and Father. To leave out either aspect is to compromise the message. We can use this principle to assess our churches and our presentation of the Gospel. At my church we saw that we were heavy on grace and light on repentance, and that this was reflected in the congregation as a lack of seriousness about sin. We needed to change our message to be in keeping with how God portrays Himself. Soon people were hearing more about repentance and there was a greater emphasis on holiness. We made a conscious choice to follow the Kingdom Way.

We rarely see Jesus speak about both characteristics of God in the same breath. What we usually see is something more toward one end of the scale or the other. The closest we come to seeing Jesus depict God as both King and Father is in the Sermon on the Mount. Take a moment to read the Sermon looking for evidence of God as King and Father. Now consider the following quick analysis of the Sermon, in which Jesus strikes an almost even balance between portraying God as King and as Father.

Matt 5:3-12	God blesses, a fatherly manifestation of His grace and generosity.
Matt 5:13-19	God expects us to be known for righteousness, an expression of one of His demands upon us as the King.
Matt 5:20-6:8	God, as the King, has a higher standard than even well informed people and wants us to know He is serious about righteousness.
Matt 6:9-13	Jesus gives the Lord's Prayer, in which God is portrayed as King and Father, and makes known His prayer requests to us.
Matt 6:14-7:6	Our Father-King has the highest standards, but is also gracious.
Matt 7:7-11	Jesus reminds us what kind of God we have, one who, though we are evil (by His kingly standard of obedience), is fatherly to give us good and gracious gifts, which we should seek and receive. (7:11)
Matt 7:12-20	Warnings and admonitions.
Matt 7:21-23	Exhortation not to forget the centrality of obedience in our response to God as King.
Matt 7:24-27	Final admonition to heed His Words.

This sermon portrays God in nearly equal measure as a King with expectations, and as a generous and gracious Father. And so it should be in our churches and in our own sharing of the Gospel. Overall we need to make sure that our message covers these two fundamental traits of God. Obviously there is room for discernment of the need of the moment so that people are told what they need to hear. Jesus did that in the examples above. But we need to strike a balance similar to the one Jesus strikes in His sermon.

Let me be clear that I am not suggesting we abandon the message of salvation by grace through faith in Jesus Christ. That is, and will always be, central to our message. My point is that *the God to Whom Jesus reconciles us* portrays Himself as King and Father. He is the one Who sent the Son. We will all reckon with Him, eventually. If our concept of the God behind Jesus is wrong, our relationship with Him will be wrong as well, perhaps so wrong as to preclude salvation. That is why it is inherent that we portray God as He portrays Himself. Much depends on it.

Prayer and the Message

But the Kingdom Way also involves prayer, and we have not really touched on that yet. As we have seen previously, every application we derive from looking at the heavenly Kingdom comes with an associated need to pray for God's intervention. Where the Gospel is concerned, we have seen that the message must include essential information about God as both King and Father, to the end that people will repent and receive grace. In this case our prayer is that people *will* come to know God as both King and Father. In view of the last chapter, we understand that it will never be enough for us to merely portray God in these ways using Scripture. We must accompany that effort with prayer, so that God's Word about Himself becomes a settled matter for them.

There is great urgency to this business of prayer. Yet in this day and age we scarcely see the importance of it. Instead we use His Word, and sort of hope something happens. We are fond of quoting the following verse to convince ourselves that we have done God's will simply by using His Word, by setting it forth:

> *So will My word be which goes forth from My mouth; It will not return to Me empty, without accomplishing what I*

desire, and without succeeding in the matter for which I sent it.
Isaiah 55:11

We say, "Well, at least they heard God's Word. You know what they say, 'it will never return empty.'" But this verse does not mean that every time *we* use God's Word that it goes forth from *Him* with power. If every use of God's Word was automatically accompanied by God's power working toward God's purposes, we would never see the devil or evil people using it for their own purposes.

On the contrary, it is when the Word goes forth from God through the Holy Spirit and right into people that it accomplishes His purposes. It must go forth from *His* mouth, by *His* Spirit. However, this does not always happen. The proof is that, in some cases, people do not respond.

> *For indeed we have had good news preached to us, just as they also; but the word they heard did not profit them, because it was not united by faith in those who heard.*
> **Hebrews 4:2**

In this case, God's Word was preached, but it did not accomplish all God's purposes. Yet, we know that…

> *The Lord is not slack concerning His promise, as some count slackness, but is longsuffering toward us, not willing that any should perish but that all should come to repentance.*
> **2 Peter 3:9**

God desires all people to come to repentance rather than perishing, yet Hebrew 4:2 shows that people do not always do so. Some do indeed perish. The full counsel of Scripture indicates that God's Word in itself does not always accomplish what He desires. With regard to salvation, it takes faith on the part of the hearer, without which nothing will happen even though the Word of God has been used.

But faith is also a gift from God.

For by grace you have been saved through faith; and that not of yourselves, it is the gift of God.
Ephesians 2:8

God often gives the gift of faith in answer to the prayers of others. George Mueller prayed for five friends all his life, and all five of them became believers, some of them after Mueller had passed away.

A new church in Scotland held services for two years without anyone coming to Christ. As soon as they started specifically asking God to save people, one or more people came to Christ each week for eight weeks in a row. This is in keeping with what Paul commands concerning prayer, that every kind of request should be brought to God.

And pray in the Spirit on all occasions with all kinds of prayers and requests.
Ephesians 6:18a

Through prayer we are to be participants *with God* in the use of His Word, rather than be merely hopeful purveyors of it. God will give the gift of faith to others when we persistently call upon Him to do so, and He will send forth His Word from us with power so that it accomplishes His purposes. He will do these things when we pray. We can call upon God with confidence that He will make Himself known as both King and Father, and that He will graciously grant people faith and repentance through our use of His Word.

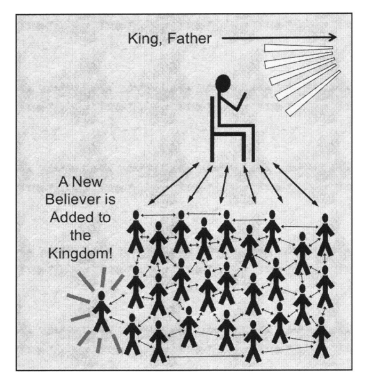

Then we will see people added to the heavenly assembly. Then people will know that Jesus came from the Father as the Savior of the world.

Challenges

God portrays Himself as King and Father. If you find either of these characteristics personally challenging, begin inventorying Scriptures that portray God in that way. Create a list of such Scriptures and then start using those in prayer, asking God to make His Word go forth in you and become an increasingly settled matter.

If the idea of God as a Father makes Him seem frightening, offensive, or repugnant, make a list of Scriptures that show He is different than your concept of what a father is like. Pray that His Word about Himself would become a settled matter for you, and be purposeful about embracing those verses as truth about Him.

If the idea of God as a King makes Him seem frightening, offensive, or repugnant, make a list of Scriptures that indicate the benefits of obeying, then answer this question: Is a King whose commands are meant to benefit me a good King or a bad King? Pray for correct understanding of God in His kingship, and that His Word about Himself would become a settled matter for you. Be purposeful about embracing those verses as truth about Him.

Study and answer this question: Is the God of the Kingdom 50% King and 50% Father, or 100% King and 100% Father? What are the implications of this?

Evaluate the way you share the Gospel. To what extent is your message faithful in portraying God as King? As Father? If you find you have been short on one characteristic of God in your presentation of the Gospel, identify three to five Scriptures you can use to strengthen that aspect of your message. Memorize them.

Identify two biblical ways in which you are refusing God as King, and repent.

Identify two biblical ways in which you are resisting God as Father, and receive His grace in those areas.

Chapter 4

Confession and Cleansing

But according to His promise we are looking for new heavens and a new earth, in which righteousness dwells. Therefore, beloved, since you look for these things, be diligent to be found by Him in peace, spotless and blameless. 2 Peter 3:13-14

In the last chapter we saw that God portrays Himself as King and Father, and that repentance from sin and receiving grace from God through Jesus are the responses that lead to salvation. Salvation on those terms gains people a place in the heavenly assembly.

In this chapter we will begin to look more closely at our relationship with Jesus in the heavens, and start to see the benefits that come from having a place in that assembly. Referring to our picture, we will be looking at the individual relationship we have with Him.

The oval I have added represents our personal relationship with Jesus. We will spend the next two chapters looking at two aspects of this relationship. In this chapter we will study the fact that those who are joined to Jesus are without unrighteousness in the heavens, and we will learn what that means for us on earth. In the next chapter, we will explore what it means for us to gain righteousness and many other things through our intimate connection with Jesus.

Righteousness Before God

One of the things Scripture teaches is that we have been *justified* before God. We have righteous standing before God because of our place before Him in Christ.

> *Therefore, having been justified by faith we have peace with God through our Lord Jesus Christ, through whom also we have obtained our introduction by faith into this grace in which we stand.*
> **Romans 5:1-2a**

Justified is a legal term. It means *made right*. In our picture, all those who have joined this assembly through the work of Jesus have been made right with God. When Jesus joined Himself with us, to make us one with Him on the cross, it was not merely to take our sins and bear the punishment for them, but also to give us His righteousness so that we could have this perfect standing before God in the heavens. So, regardless of the fact that we still sin on earth, there are no unrighteous people before God among those who have been joined to Jesus in the heavens. And that is what we see in this verse:

> *Blessed be the God and Father of our Lord Jesus Christ, who has blessed us with every spiritual blessing in the heavenly places in Christ, just as He chose us in Him before the foundation of the world, that we would be holy and blameless before Him.*
> **Ephesians 1:3-4a**

We are holy and blameless before God. This allows us to define another of the Things Above: That we are without any unrighteousness before God in the heavens. One of the Things Above is you, righteous, blameless! And from what we know about the Kingdom Way, we can expect that for God's will to be done on earth as in heaven, there must be a way for us to be blameless here on earth. That sounds like something we would all want.

However, all this talk about unrighteousness among believers may raise concerns among some readers. You may feel that I am going to say unbiblical things that diminish the amazing work that Jesus has done for us. I assure you this is not the case. But you may have this verse jumping up in your mind:

> *Therefore if anyone is in Christ, he is a new creature; the old things passed away; behold, new things have come.*
> **2 Corinthians 5:17**

I agree with this verse wholeheartedly. We are new creations in Christ. This chapter is about how we learn to live as though that is true and obtain all the good things we are meant to have as new creations. So, let me first clear up a couple things.

First, as the Kingdom Way emphasizes, we need to be aware that just because something is true in the heavens does not mean it will automatically be worked out on earth in the present. The Kingdom Way teaches us to look at the Things Above and model some response on what we see there. We also accompany that response with prayer to bring God's miraculous intervention into play, so there is fruit. It is the same in the case of unrighteousness. Just because we see our righteousness in the heavens does not mean that we will automatically possess it here. We will have some involvement in seeing it happen here, and that involvement will include prayer. In this case, there is a real thing called unrighteousness that we can possess here on earth that, of course, we cannot possess in heaven. God wants us to be free of it. The Kingdom Way will show us how.

Second, these days there is not, generally, a good idea what unrighteousness is, and without a good idea what it is we are in danger of possessing it without even knowing that we do. Believers can have unrighteousness despite being saved, despite having the righteousness of Jesus in heaven. One of the goals of this chapter is to provide a clear understanding of what unrighteousness is, what it does to us, and how God has provided a way to get rid it.

The First Discipline of the Christian Life

To learn more about unrighteousness, we will need a good bit of background in the area of confession. Consider this scene with John the Baptist, when he was preaching the Kingdom of God.

> *And so John the Baptist appeared in the wilderness, preaching a baptism of repentance for the forgiveness of sins. The whole Judean countryside and all the people of Jerusalem went out to him. Confessing their sins, they were baptized by him in the Jordan River.*
> **Mark 1:4-5**

As people came they were confessing their sins. Whether or not this was a guided response, it certainly seems to be something that was both important in the context of John's ministry, and worth mentioning by Mark in his writing of the Gospel. In fact, we can view confession as the first discipline that is encouraged in a new believer's life.[5] Understanding confession is the precursor to understanding unrighteousness, so we will take some time to examine biblical confession in detail. Also, the Kingdom Way comes into play where confession itself is concerned, and we will see how that happens as well.

Now, if we are going to go about things the Kingdom Way in our preaching, we must also be prepared to guide people toward the appropriate response, which includes confession of sins. First century Jews may have had a good idea what confession was, but today there is little certainty that we, or people in our churches, have any clear idea what it is. For this reason we need to look at confession in greater detail, making sure we understand what it is and why we need to do it.

But let's have a definition first. What exactly is confession? The word comes from two Greek words, *homo*, meaning "same", and *logeo*,

---

[5] For the record, baptism is not a discipline. It is a one-time matter of obedience.

meaning "to speak" or "to say". So then, to confess is to say the same thing. Picture someone in court, being questioned on the stand. The prosecutor might ask, "Did you kill the Colonel in the kitchen with the candlestick?" A confession would be "Yes, I killed the Colonel in the kitchen with the candlestick." The accused would be saying the same thing as the prosecutor, owning up to the murder by confessing it.

In a biblical context, to confess means to say the same thing *as God*. Where do we find what God says? In His Word. Confession, therefore, refers to God's Word and says about our sins the same thing God says about them. Confession is agreeing with God by measuring our sins according to His Word.

Of course, we've seen that before. In chapter two we talked about God's Word as the measure of our lives. God's Word is one of the Things Above. His will is being done on earth as in heaven when it becomes increasingly the measure of our lives. Confessing a sin as measured by God's Word is also God's will being done on earth as in heaven because it is the response of one for whom the Word has become a more settled matter. Thus, it is no surprise to see John guiding people toward that response while he preaches the Kingdom of God.

But was confessing sins in reference to God's Word a new thing in John's day? No. In fact there are multiple examples of it in the Old Testament. One of the clearest comes from Nehemiah.

> *When I heard these things, I sat down and wept. For some days I mourned and fasted and prayed before the God of heaven. Then I said: "O LORD, God of heaven, the great and awesome God, who keeps his covenant of love with those who love him and obey his commands, let your ear be attentive and your eyes open to hear the prayer your servant is praying before you day and night for your servants, the people of Israel. I confess the sins we Israelites, including myself and my father's house, have committed against you. We have acted very wickedly toward you. We have not obeyed the commands, decrees and laws you gave your servant Moses.*
> **Nehemiah 1:4-7**

Nehemiah was the cupbearer to king Darius of Babylon. He was praying for three months in preparation to go before this great king and make an enormous request. He was asking God for favor prior to doing so. What we see in this passage is a summary of his last prayer, right before he goes in to see king Darius. In this prayer we find him confessing sins for himself and on behalf of Israel. Note that God's law, and disobedience to it, were central to Nehemiah's confession. Nehemiah knew that sins are measured by specifics in God's Word. His view of confession was consistent with what we have seen about God's Word being settled in heaven, and being the measure of our lives and actions on earth.

In fact, God's Word must be the measure of our sins. Without a standard reference point outside ourselves, our concept of sin will be skewed and inadequate. We can sin without regret. We can sin without recognizing harm to others or ourselves. We can even sin without realizing it at the time. But our sins are not measured by the harm they have done others or ourselves, nor by our regrets, nor by our feelings. These may all help us recognize our sins, but the real measure of our sins is the Word of God, and our confession should be that our sinful actions represent a departure from that Word.

God's Word proceeds out of His holiness, and His holiness is infinite. Though the suffering we have caused may exceed our ability to measure it, it is still less than the offense we have done to God in living contrary to His holiness. David knew this even when it came to his sin with Bathsheba and the murder of her husband.

> *Against you, you only, have I sinned and done what is evil in your sight; so you are right in your verdict and justified when you judge.*
> **Psalm 51:4**

God's Word is also a better measure of our sin than our feelings. Our feelings can mislead us. Our consciences can become seared and our actions can become so justified in our own sight that we have no pangs of guilt or remorse about our sins. But the Word of God stands forever as a settled matter, unchanging. It continuously calls us to live God's way. It is an objective measure that has been given to us to retrain our consciences, so that even where our consciences have become seared we may be set free and return to harmony with God. As Paul wrote to Timothy:

> *All Scripture is God-breathed and is useful for teaching, rebuking, correcting and training in righteousness so that the servant of God may be thoroughly equipped for every good work.*
> **2 Timothy 3:16-17**

So, we are to be trained in righteousness by the Word of God. One of the ways this happens is to develop a healthy discipline of confessing our sins as measured by His Word regardless of whether we feel any guilt or not. Such a discipline forces us back to His Word, makes us more familiar with it, and ultimately should help us be more surrendered to it. When this happens God's Word is going forth, as we have discussed. It is going forth within us and becoming a more settled matter.

Confession of Individual Sins

Notice also from the passages we have examined that it is always sins, plural, that are confessed. In John's ministry, they came "confessing their sins." Nehemiah confessed his sins and the sins of his people. This is true nearly everywhere we see confession of sins in the Bible. Confession is of specific sins, plural, not sin patterns or sin as a generality. A pattern of sin in our lives is really just a product of all the similar individual sins we have committed in violation of God's Word. But it is individual sins of which we are guilty, not the pattern they form.

Consider an example. Let's say you are speeder. You speed quite often. One day you are pulled over for going really fast and are ticketed. You have to appear in court. Are you in court because you are a speeder, or are you there because on a certain date at a certain time in a certain place you sped by a certain amount? The officer and the court are unaware that you speed frequently. All they know is that you were speeding when you got caught. It was the single, specific violation that got you hauled in to court. You violated the law while driving and were brought to court for it. It was not the pattern that landed you in court. It was the one violation for which you were caught.

So it is with God. It is individual sins that are the concern of confession. But there's a difference between speeding and sinning against God. When we speed the police do not always catch us. However, when we sin against God by violating His Word we are always caught by God. Paul makes this clear when he mentions transgressions, plural, and decrees, plural, against us. These are our individual sins.

> *When you were dead in your transgressions and the uncircumcision of your flesh, He made you alive together with Him, having forgiven us all our transgressions, having canceled out the certificate of debt consisting of decrees against us, which was hostile to us; and He has taken it out of the way, having nailed it to the cross.*
> **Colossians 2:13-15**

What we want to notice in these verses is that God thinks of our sins individually, not as some indistinguishable mass, or general pattern of sin. He sees each sin specifically, and has done through Jesus what was necessary to cancel the decree of debt associated with each individual sin, and establish a relationship with us in the heavens, one in which we have no unrighteousness before Him.

This way of thinking is contrary to the way some of us have been taught. Many of us think that we have a problem with sin, generally, or a pattern of sinning of some type. We often think of it this way: "I have SIN," or, if the sin issue looms large in our minds, we may think our problem is…

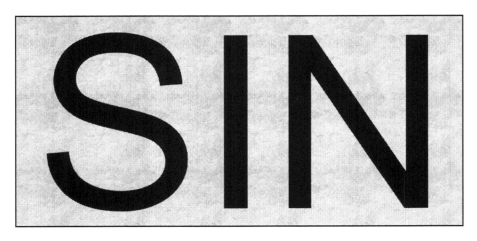

…in big, capital letters. This is how we commonly think about patterns of sin in our lives. We are inclined to talk to God about our "sin," hoping He will change us, as though that is biblical confession. But the biblical view is that a pattern of sin is actually made up of many individual occurrences of sins, without which there would be no pattern.[6] The next picture shows how individual sins create a pattern that we often simply refer to as our sin.

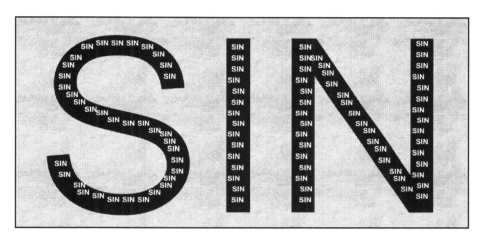

But when it comes to sins, God measures our transgressions one by one, and each one is a violation serious enough for a decree against us (see Colossians 2:13-15, above). Since this is the case, when it comes to confession, it is no longer the pattern that matters. Rather, it is the individual sins themselves.

---

[6] I am not saying that we do not have a sin nature. We do. What I am saying is that there is a difference between a pattern of individual sins that we think of as SIN, and our sin nature. Our sin nature is a law at work within all of us that is a root cause of sinfulness (see Romans 8:2). Patterns of sin are the result of the sin nature manifesting itself through many individual sins.

When we are guilty of a sin, it is because we are guilty of specifically acting contrary to God's Word in a certain way on a particular occasion, like the person that speeds and ends up in court. So a more accurate way of talking about a pattern of sin would be to say, "I have committed these sins," or, "I often commit sins of this sort." Sin (the generality) is a pattern of individual offenses, but as a pattern, it is not "confessable" in the biblical sense, because it is our individual sins that are considered transgressions. So it is individual sins, not sin patterns, or sin generally, that we are to confess. And this is what we see as the response to John's message. It was sins, plural, that people confessed:

The whole Judean countryside and all the people of Jerusalem went out to him. Confessing their sins, they were baptized by him in the Jordan River.
Mark 1:5

When people come to repentance for the first time, the sins they confess are often the so-called "big ones," things like immorality, murder, stealing, drunkenness, betrayal, violence, greed, lying, hatred, abuse, and the like. These are sins that are obvious to them even though they have not been trained much in righteousness by the Word of God. Over time, as we are trained by the Word going forth within us, our sensitivity to sin should increase. We should become sensitive to wrong attitudes, subtle rejections of authority, unholy thoughts, refusals to believe the Scriptures and other sins.

Biblical confession is specific to individual sins, measures them by God's Word, and is meant to be thorough *and regular*. A believer with a good discipline of confession will confess sins as they occur. However, without regularly and thoroughly confessing sins, a believer can build up quite a backlog of sins that need to be confessed.

Cleansing Through Confession

What is the benefit of all this confessing? The short answer is that it is critical to spiritual growth and progress in overcoming sin. In the beginning of the chapter, I discussed God's desire that we should be without unrighteousness here on earth, just as we are without it in the heavens. But we still don't have a good idea what unrighteousness is, where it comes from, or what role confession plays in all this. It is time we found out.

It turns out that sin always gets us two things we don't want. The first is objective, factual guilt before God. Sinning results in decrees against us, and incurs the judgment of God. For believers, those judgments have been cancelled, taken out of the way by Jesus when He died on the cross. There are no longer decrees of judgment against us, because the work of Christ covers the sins of our entire lives. All of them, even ones in the future, were cancelled by the far-reaching power of Jesus' sacrifice. We have been justified, made right. So for believers there is no longer objective guilt that incurs judgment from God.

The second thing we get from sinning is unrighteousness here on earth. What is unrighteousness? Unrighteousness is a harmful spiritual substance that is produced every time we sin, and that clings to us afterward as a result. Just as objective guilt accrues to us and is a real thing that can be forgiven through the blood of Christ, unrighteousness is a real thing that accrues to us on earth as a result of sins. Simplistically, we can think of unrighteousness as spiritual dirt left over from sins. However, as we will see, there is much to learn about unrighteousness and its effect on us. It is not a simple matter.

Where do we learn about unrighteousness in the Scriptures? John writes:

If we confess our sins, He is faithful and righteous to forgive us our sins and to cleanse us from all unrighteousness.
I John 1:9

John distinguishes forgiveness and cleansing. Forgiveness deals with objective guilt before God. Cleansing, which comes through confession, deals with unrighteousness. This verse makes it clear that guilt from sin is a different thing from unrighteousness, and that they have different remedies. Sin requires forgiveness; unrighteousness requires cleansing, obtained through confession.

However, in common usage, the word unrighteousness is so strongly associated with sin itself that we do not generally see it as a separate thing from a sinful act, pattern, or lifestyle. But it is an important distinction to make. Sinfulness is characterized by sinful actions and thoughts, whereas unrighteousness is characterized by an unseen quality of iniquity, however subtle, that seasons our souls with impurity. Since an incorrect concept of unrighteousness is an obstacle to understanding what cleansing is all about, I prefer to call it *residual* unrighteousness, which emphasizes that is it something left over after a sin, rather than a sin itself.

How do we know if we have residual unrighteousness? The answer is that our consciences let us know. Residual unrighteousness results in consciousness of sins we have committed. We are aware that we have done something wrong, and our consciences remind us of that from time to time. Paul sheds light on this in Romans.

For when Gentiles who do not have the Law do instinctively the things of the Law, these, not having the Law, are a law to themselves, in that they show the work of the Law written in their hearts, their conscience bearing witness and their thoughts alternately accusing or else defending them.
Romans 2:14-15

Paul is saying that when our conscience accuses us, it is evidence of a sin we have committed. The conscience points out our residual unrighteousness. Granted, Paul is writing about unbelieving Gentiles, but the principle holds true for everyone. The only difference is that believers have forgiveness and a means to obtain cleansing from residual unrighteousness, whereas unbelievers do not.

But there is an even better passage that discusses the conscience, and the cleansing that is available to us through Christ. In Hebrews 9:1-10:22, the writer provides a long argument about conscience and our consciousness of sins. The passage discusses the superiority of Christ's ministry over the temple worship and sacrifices of the Old Testament. Easily missed amongst all the Old Testament references and history are several mentions of the conscience, and consciousness of sins. These phrases actually make up the main theme of the passage.

The teaching begins by recalling the articles of worship and the practices of the priests and the high priest. The high priest entered the Most Holy Place only once a year, bringing offerings for the people. Then the author states…

> *Accordingly both gifts and sacrifices are offered which cannot make the worshiper **perfect in conscience**, since they relate only to food and drink and various washings, regulations for the body imposed until a time of reformation.*
> **Hebrews 9:9b-10**

The temple sacrifices were incapable of cleansing the consciences of the people. However, in the next section we are told that Jesus has entered the greater tabernacle, one not made with hands (v. 11), which is the very presence of God in the heavens. The author points out that if the blood of bulls and goats sufficed to provide cleansing of the flesh, that is, ceremonial cleansing that permitted one to minister in the tabernacle…

> *how much more will the blood of Christ, who through the eternal Spirit offered Himself without blemish to God, **cleanse your conscience** from dead works to serve the living God?*
> **Hebrews 9:14**

This verse makes clear that cleansing of our consciences is something God wants us to obtain through the blood of Christ. In the rest of the chapter, the writer contrasts the earthly sacrificial practices prescribed in the Law with the perfect work of Jesus in sanctifying the heavenly things with His own blood. The writer follows with these words.

> *For the Law, since it has only a shadow of the good things to come and not the very form of things, can never, by the same sacrifices which they offer continually year by year, make perfect those who draw near. Otherwise, would they not have ceased to be offered, because the worshipers, having once **been cleansed**, would no longer have had **consciousness of sins?***
> **Hebrews 10:1-2**

Again, freedom from consciousness of sins we've committed is God's will for us, but it was not available through the Old Testament sacrificial system. This is not to say that God wants us to be unaware that we sin. Rather, He desires that we not carry through our lives the burden of our accusing consciences speaking to us incessantly about past sins. When we have consciousness of sins, we are in need of the cleansing that God wants to provide. And, as we noted, 1 John 1:9 indicates that cleansing comes through confession.

As the writer goes on, he flips repeatedly to a heavenly perspective, using language that describes our connection with Jesus in His work of perfecting us. The author establishes that there is now a new covenant through Christ that provides sanctification for all those who are saved, pointing out that...

> *... by one offering He has perfected for all time those who are sanctified.*
> **Hebrews 10:14**

The context makes clear that the author is referring to our sanctification in the presence of God in the heavens. He is discussing the Things Above. Starting in verse nineteen the author leaves the Things Above behind and gets to the application of the whole discourse. Here is what he writes.

> *Therefore, brethren, since we have confidence to enter the holy place by the blood of Jesus, by a new and living way which He inaugurated for us through the veil, that is, His flesh, and since we have a great priest over the house of*

*God, let us **draw near with a sincere heart** in full assurance of faith, having our **hearts sprinkled clean from an evil conscience** and our bodies washed with pure water.* **Hebrews 10:19-22**

The author has reverted to the earthly perspective. This is clear because he is now addressing his brethren, advising them to draw near[7] to God, and have their *hearts sprinkled clean from an evil conscience*. This is the cleansing that God wants to give us, which we can have if we draw near. However, we will miss out on cleansing if we disobey this admonition by refusing to draw near.

Where is confession in this passage? To *draw near with a sincere heart* encompasses confession and many other ways of addressing God through prayer. In fact, there is hardly a more sincere way of speaking to God than agreeing with Him about how our sinful actions have failed to measure up to the standard of His Word. That is what confession is – frank and sincere talk with God about our individual sins, in which we agree with Him in what He says about them.

A Case Study

But this is still too abstract, I fear. Let me tell you my own story of how biblical confession and cleansing from unrighteousness transformed my life.

Some years ago I noticed my spiritual growth had begun to seem limited. I knew how to abide in Christ, and had a good balance of study, prayer, fellowship, and service, but I was still not able to beat certain sins in my life, and I didn't know why. I realized I had believed God only for His great power toward me. That was good, but I had not believed Him for "the *surpassing* greatness of His power toward us who believe" (Ephesians 1:19.) So I prayed, acknowledged my unbelief as a sin, repented, and waited for Him to lead me. Through various means, He led me to the idea of confessing every sin I remembered. I did not yet understand cleansing, but I knew that I had

---

[7] Note that the writer is not telling his brethren to get saved. He addresses them as brethren. They are already saved. He is telling them something they should do because of their salvation.

a lot of sins to confess. I remember thinking "We're going to be here a while."

But I started. It took a very long time, several months. Since I had not had a good discipline of biblical confession prior to this time, I had quite a large backlog of sins to confess. But as I confessed them, I found that He met me with cleansing for each one.

What was that like? For each sin I confessed, I received a sense of relief and peace about the matter. I gained a sense of joy along with assurance that the sin had indeed been forgiven. I also found that I no longer had to think about that sin. It was gone, done. Confessed sins became forgettable because my conscience no longer prodded me about them. I soon forgot most of them. In fact for more than 99% of them, I can't remember them at all now. My consciousness of the sins I had committed went away, which was an immense relief.

What I experienced was far more than psychological healing. I had remembered many of those sins for years, yet, once cleansing came, the memory of them quickly faded. I am now convinced that it was residual unrighteousness far more than my own natural memory that kept those sins coming to mind year after year. Remember that residual unrighteousness is a spiritual substance that clings to us. It is specific to the sins we have committed, and our consciences are sensitive to it. When cleansing comes, residual unrighteousness disappears, and the memory of the sin can fade.

The Holy Spirit met me with sanctifying power at each and every point of confession. Images in my mind from various sources, impure sexual images from movies and print, scenes from a horror film I had watched, all these were removed from me through cleansing that came as a result of confession.

I was also healed of a painful memory that came from witnessing an act of brutality that I had nothing to do with. What does that have to do with confession? Remember that confession means to say the same thing as God says. My confession was to say the same thing about it that He said. It *was* sad and painful and tragic. I spoke with Him sincerely (Hebrews 10:19-22) about how painful and sad the event and the memories were. He came alongside me with His empathy for me, He cleansed the pain of it away, and the memories soon faded. I've experienced similar healing for regrets as well, simply by talking sincerely and frankly with God about them. The Fatherly love of God proves to be a restorative balm when we talk with Him sincerely about our cares.

Even more astonishingly, Jesus completely set me free from the tendency to sin in some ways, which can only be described as having been set free from slavery to those sins. My susceptibility to other sins was greatly reduced.

Let me be perfectly clear: There is not one area of my life that failed to improve as a result of specific, thorough, biblical confession of sins. The result was transformative. My readiness to see the surpassing greatness of God's power toward me was fulfilled far beyond all I could ask or imagine. The change that took place in me over those several months was nothing less than a major spiritual renewal, easily ranking among the most significant events of my spiritual life.

Confession in Practice

Few people approach confession this way. Usually, if people attempt to confess anything at all, they dwell in generalities and talk about their patterns. But as we have discussed already, that is not biblical confession. Biblical confession deals with specific sins and measures them by the Word of God.

When I began my season of confession, I had already begun to understand some aspects of the Kingdom of God and how God wants us to go about things. I knew that measuring our lives by God's Word was central. So when I approached a sin to confess it, let's say anger about something, I kept the Word of God close at hand. I had several verses about anger that I had looked up ahead of time and written on cards, or memorized. Using one of them to measure my sin, I confessed the individual sin of anger to God by stating exactly what I had done, thought, said, or wished, focusing on the anger aspect of it, and how it was wrong as measured by His Word. I would read or state the verse in prayer as part of my confession, wholly owning that I was guilty of disobeying His Word, and that it was sin.[8] After confessing

---

[8] I didn't typically ask for forgiveness, because that is not the same as confession. Asking forgiveness is requesting something from God.

the sin, I thanked God for His forgiveness and for cleansing me from my unrighteousness. At that point, it was often apparent that cleansing had taken place, because my guilty conscience about the matter was removed.

In some cases confessing a sin like anger also required me to forgive someone that had sinned against me. If that was the case, I dealt with God about that as well, confessing my unforgiveness as an additional sin according to His Word, and repenting of that by forgiving the person. James 1:3 also says that trials come into our lives as a means of testing our faith and producing endurance. I found that sometimes my anger was about a circumstance that was meant to test my faith and produce endurance, and I had to confess that I had accused God of being absent in the midst of a trial, or worse, being uncaring or wrong in letting it into my life. The truth is that God was always both present and righteous in allowing such circumstances into my life. My anger was unjustified and sinful.

These additional layers of complexity were less rare than I like to admit. They became apparent when my conscience still prodded me about something related to the event; instead of experiencing complete cleansing that removed consciousness of the sin, I found I was still thinking about some aspect of it. The Holy Spirit was a big help in searching my heart and leading me in these things, and while it was often painful, it was well worth it.

Confession is a statement. It is agreeing with God about a sin in light of His Word. When cleansing came, it provided evidence that I *was* forgiven, whether I had asked for it or not. In fact, Ephesians 1:7 and Colossians 1:14 both state that we *have redemption, the forgiveness of sins*. We don't need to ask for forgiveness. We can stand in faith on those verses and *know* that we have it.

However, it is critically important not to equate forgiveness and cleansing. There is a tendency among believers to ask for forgiveness for a sin without ever having fully owned up to our sinfulness in committing it. We can skip the part where we humble ourselves. When we do that we can miss out on the benefit of cleansing. But when cleansing comes through biblical confession it *proves* we are forgiven, *even without having asked for forgiveness*. Receiving cleansing is meant to be a powerful reminder of God's grace that increases our thankfulness toward Him.

Once I began confessing my sins and started experiencing cleansing, I realized I had experienced it before. Chances are good that many of you have experienced cleansing without realizing it, as well. In my life, there had been times I had sinned, felt intensely ashamed, and had gone to God in confession. He had met me with grace and a sense of relief about the sins I had committed, and my conscience didn't bother me about them anymore. That was cleansing. He did this despite the fact that I knew nothing about cleansing at the time. He was faithful to honor His promise when I spoke to Him frankly and humbly about my sins, whether I understood what He was doing or not.

When you begin this journey, it is important to resist the temptation to go through diaries or journals to dig up past sins. If you still have residual unrighteousness, your conscience and the Holy Spirit will let you to know about the related sins. A journey of confession is not meant to be a morose review of our lives. Rather it is to be a time of drawing nearer to God and experiencing the sweetness of His grace through cleansing.

Confession and Cleansing in Kingdom Terms

We've said much about the relationship between confession and cleansing but if we can't see the Kingdom Way in this, it is likely we'll lose sight of it as something God wants for us, or at least not be able to teach it very effectively. What is actually going on when we confess a sin? We are admitting that an earthly action of ours failed to measure up to God's heavenly Word. That in itself is God's will being done on earth as in heaven, because we are treating God's heavenly Word as a settled matter here on earth. His Word is going forth in us, just as He wants.

In response to our confession of a sin, God takes the blood of Christ, which Jesus took into the heavenly sanctuary (Hebrews 9:14, 10:22), and sprinkles it on our soul right at the point of the related residual unrighteousness. He cleanses us at that exact point. He takes the blood that purified us in heaven forever and applies it to us on earth at the specific place where our residual unrighteousness is lodged in us. The result is that the purity we have before God in the heavens is given to us on earth, removing the residual unrighteousness on a sin-by-sin basis as we confess. This also achieves God's will on earth as in heaven, because God means for us to be pure here, as we are there.

We can view the process like this:

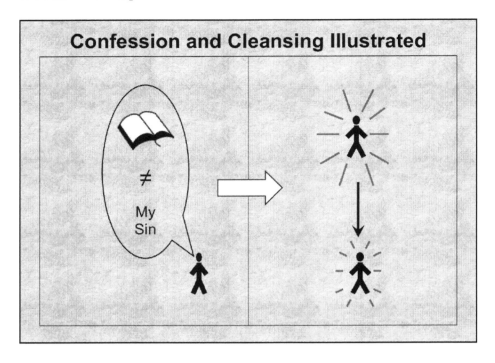

In the illustration, the believer is confessing a sin, admitting that it did not measure up to God's heavenly Word. Next, the purity he has in the heavens is given to him on earth. The residual unrighteousness he had is gone, having been cleansed away.

Confession and cleansing both fit into our understanding of the Kingdom of God. It is only because of our poor understanding of confession and our unawareness of our need for cleansing that we have needed to talk so long about what is actually a simple and beautiful process.

Notice that we haven't specifically talked about prayer as the key to seeing God's will done on earth as in heaven as we did in previous chapters. Although that is a critical component of living by the Kingdom, we haven't needed to made that linkage in this case because confession *is* the prayer that brings about God's will on earth when He cleanses us.

The Power of Residual Unrighteousness

When I went through my season of confession, I experienced deliverance from certain sins and noticed a significant boost in my ability to combat others. How did that happen? As it turns out, residual unrighteousness from past sins has the ability to incline us toward sins of the same type. It becomes harder and harder to resist those sins because we have engaged in them so many times before, every time accumulating residual unrighteousness as a result. So even though I am not by nature personally prone to much anger, the numerous times I had sinned in anger, and not confessed the sins, had resulted in a buildup of residual unrighteousness that made it easier and more likely for me to sin in anger as years went by. Once I confessed those sins and the residual unrighteousness was gone, I found that I simply didn't have much tendency to get angry anymore.

However, confessing sins of anger did not gain me any freedom with regard to, say, selfishness. Apparently residual unrighteousness is specific to the type of sin committed. Someone who confesses a great many sins of greed, and sees the benefits of that in being less greedy, will find little or no relief in the area of lust until that area is dealt with as well.

Unconfessed sin permits residual unrighteousness to remain in us and cause us problems. It is not that we are unforgiven. Everyone that has entered the Kingdom of God has been made one with Christ in the heavens, and that is not a place where unforgiven people get to be. But it is not in keeping with our heavenly purity to live with the impurity of residual unrighteousness here on earth. Residual unrighteousness causes us pain through our consciences, is a hindrance to righteous living, and diminishes our enjoyment of God. In contrast, confession brings to light what is hidden in darkness and humbles us. Confession honors God in His holiness, and creates an opportunity for Him to lift us up through cleansing.

Residual unrighteousness also hinders our prayers.

> *If I regard wickedness in my heart,*
> *The Lord will not hear*
> **Psalm 66:18**

But cleansing reverses the damage, strengthening our prayers.

> *Beloved, if our heart does not condemn us, we have confidence before God; and whatever we ask we receive from Him, because we keep His commandments and do the things that are pleasing in His sight.*
> **1 John 3:21-22**

But is it True?

Before we go on let us take stock of what we have seen and have a look around the Scriptures, as we've done before, to make sure what we've discussed is actually biblical. Here are the main points we've covered, reordered in a more logical way.

- Every sin results in some residual unrighteousness.
- Residual unrighteousness is a harmful spiritual substance that clings to us.
- It has power to incline us toward similar sins.
- It can accumulate.
- Consciousness of sins committed is an indicator of residual unrighteousness.
- We are meant to have a clean conscience, to be free from consciousness of sins committed.
- We are meant to be free from the power of residual unrighteousness to incline us toward similar sins.
- God will cleanse us from residual unrighteousness when we biblically confess a sin.
- Biblical confession of a sin is saying the same thing God says about it in His Word, admitting it was a sin as measured by His Word.
- Confession is of individual sins, not of sin patterns or our sinful nature.
- Thorough, specific, biblical confession of individual sins is one part of successful repentance.
- Confession of sins is the first discipline taught to new believers, and is meant to be a regular part of our lives.
- Confession and cleansing strengthen our prayer life.

We won't cover all these points as we review the Scriptures. Some of them have been covered adequately above, but here is an interesting verse that fits with what we have seen about residual unrighteousness.

> *Repent and turn away from all your transgressions, so that iniquity may not become a stumbling block to you.*
> **Ezekiel 18:30**

In this verse, Ezekiel urges the hearers to repent from sins (transgressions) so that iniquity won't become a stumbling block. Iniquity generally has two meanings; one is "a lack of justice or righteousness; wickedness, injustice." The other is "a wicked act; sin."[9] Looking back at the verse, if we substitute "a wicked act", or "sin" in place of iniquity, Ezekiel would essentially be saying "so that a sin won't become a cause of sin," which doesn't make much sense. However if we see iniquity as "a lack of righteousness" or as "unrighteousness," the verse makes much more sense. Ezekiel would then be saying "Repent and turn away from all your sins, so that unrighteousness may not cause you to fall into sin." This is in perfect agreement with what we have seen about residual unrighteousness and its power to incline us toward similar sins. Ezekiel is telling them to repent so they don't build up residual unrighteousness (iniquity) that pushes them into additional sin.

David also shows a keen understanding of the need for cleansing and the role of his conscience. In Psalm 51, written about his sins concerning Bathsheba and Uriah, David writes these words:

> *Wash away all my iniquity and cleanse me from my sin.*
> *For I know my transgressions, and my sin is always before me.*
> **Psalm 51:2-3**

David's conscience was prodding him to go to God and make this sincere prayer because he was experiencing consciousness of sins. The entire psalm echoes with his plea for God to relieve his guilty conscience and restore his joy.

Jeremiah also makes a distinction between cleansing and forgiveness.

---

[9] World English Dictionary

I will cleanse them from all the sin they have committed against me, and will forgive all their sins of rebellion against me.
Jeremiah 33:8

Paul also instructs Timothy about cleansing. In a discourse against quarreling, godless chatter, and false teaching (2 Timothy 2:14-21) he draws this analogy.

In a large house there are articles not only of gold and silver, but also of wood and clay; some are for special purposes and some for common use. Those who cleanse themselves from the latter will be instruments for special purposes, made holy, useful to the Master and prepared to do any good work.
2 Timothy 2:20-21

Paul could have simply said "those who *rid* themselves of the latter," but instead chose the word "cleanse." Paul's point in the passage is that being cleansed of sins involving speech can make the difference between being like some ordinary object and being one of significant value, holy and useful to the Lord. If we consider James' teaching on the tongue (James 3:8) and how hard it is to tame, we can understand why Paul would use the word cleanse, rather than rid. All of us sin with our tongues. But those who make effort to be cleansed of residual unrighteousness will be much less likely to fall in their speech than those who don't. Since our speech is such an important means of communicating the things of God, this is a critical area to address.

Cleansing and the Big Picture

There is a bigger picture to confession and cleansing, however. When we look back at Jesus' prayer in John 17, we recall that the reason He wanted us to be one with Him was so that the world would know that He had come from God. Everything that comes out of our union with Christ in the heavens is to have some impact on the world, and help provide credible evidence of Jesus as the Savior. Cleansing is to have that impact in several ways.

Consider these implications for your own life. By regularly receiving cleansing through disciplined confession, you would also be regularly receiving proof of God's forgiveness. You would obtain freedom from troubling images that may have been in your mind for years. You would be freer from the power of sin, because you would no longer have residual unrighteousness continuously inclining you toward it. You would likely be completely delivered from some sins. You would have hope, because the words of victory you read in the New Testament would begin to ring true to your own experience. Your familiarity with the Scriptures would also increase, because you would learn verses to use in your confessions.

You would gain confidence about the other Things Above because you would see God acting immediately on His promise of cleansing. You would be motivated by your understanding of residual unrighteousness to be rid of it as quickly as possible, which in turn would fuel a healthier and more regular prayer life. Receiving cleansing soon after sinning would also bolster your appreciation for God's grace, His desire to strengthen you, and His determination to make you holy. You would be more joyful, and you would have a stronger testimony of God's work in your life because of all the benefits you receive through cleansing.

In all these things, your life would provide better evidence of Jesus as the Savior, and you would begin to see that Peter's assertion is true.

> *His divine power has given us everything we need for a godly life through our knowledge of him who called us by his own glory and goodness. Through these he has given us his very great and precious promises, so that through them you may participate in the divine nature, having escaped the corruption in the world caused by evil desires.*
> **2 Peter 1:3-4**

God wants you to be set free from sin's power. He means for you to experience His grace through cleansing. He wants believers to have a testimony of His work in their lives. And He means for all of this to point to Jesus as the Savior. God has indeed given us everything we need for life and godliness through His promises. The promise of confession and cleansing is just one of these provisions. It is designed for our edification and His glorification, things we can expect to come about when we correctly understand His present day Kingdom.

Challenges

Choose one area of sin in your life that you will begin to tackle through confession. Find five verses or passages that address that sin. Write these on cards or memorize them. Begin confessing sins using the following prayer. It is a good model prayer that incorporates the key elements of a confession.

> Father, that time when I sinned by _____ (specifically recount the sin you are confessing), I went against your Word, which says _____ (read or quote one of the relevant verses.) I wholly confess that I was wrong to disobey you in that way. Thank you for your forgiveness and cleansing.

Continue confessing sins until you have completed a thorough confession for that area of your life. Feel free to be flexible in your conversation with God as long as you are careful to incorporate the key elements of confession.

After confessing numerous sins in one area, pause and reflect on your consciousness of the sins you have confessed. Do you notice a difference? Can you sense that cleansing has taken place?

After making a thorough confession of one area of your life, spend a short period of up to a few days praising and thanking God before moving on to another area. It is good to rest periodically and refresh ourselves.

Once you begin a new area of your life, you may recall additional sins from the first area of your life. Confess them but don't return to dwelling on that first area. Keep pressing on with the next area of your life, to complete it. It is ordinary for us not to remember every sin of a certain type the first time through. The goal is to complete a thorough confession of your backlog of unconfessed sins, but it does not have to be perfect on the first pass. The goal is to *reduce your total burden* of residual unrighteousness *as quickly as possible*, so getting the easily remembered ones first makes strategic sense. There is time to mop up the remaining sins afterward.

Move on through all the main areas of your life confessing every sin you can bring to mind. The point is not to obsess over past sins, but rather to allow the Holy Spirit to prompt your conscience about things in the past that you have not yet brought to God in confession.

If you need to reconcile with others, do it. There is not much point in confessing sins only to add to our sins by resisting the Scriptures on this point. Do not harden your heart to one sin while endeavoring to honor God with the rest of your life.

Listen to audio Bible on CD or on your iPod for extended periods over the course of several weeks. As the Word of God goes forth in you, you may find past sins coming to mind. This is the power of the Word of God to bring to light areas in need of confession and repentance. Take note of them and work through them with confession and repentance. Don't be discouraged; this is a temporary phenomenon. Once you have dealt with these things they won't likely crop up again. You will notice that if you deal with these areas through confession and repentance, further Bible listening will not bring them to mind again.

Draft a strategy in writing for how to guide a new believer toward confession when they have come to God for salvation. If they have a natural inclination to confess their sins, encourage this and support them in it as long as they are willing to continue. At the end of their confession, explain that their joy is due to God cleansing them from unrighteousness from their sins, and that confession is a normal and regular thing believers do. Explain also that the joy and release they have is evidence that God has forgiven them.

If you are a teacher or pastor, prayerfully plan how you will lead those in your care toward confession and cleansing. Remember that not everyone is interested in, or able to receive, the full theological scope of this teaching, but all are meant to benefit from confession and cleansing. Form your strategy with prayer and with sensitivity to peoples' interest level. Recognize that the importance of this discipline must be reinforced on regular intervals. Consider teaching a series on this, followed by teaching every two months until people begin to get it, then no less than every three months, to make sure everyone that newly attends also learns this important discipline. Your own testimony about cleansing will be critical to making the case. Guide people toward the verses they will need to use in their confessions, or turn them toward online Bible search engines like Biblegateway.com. Solicit testimonies from others about their experiences with cleansing. Share them with your groups, anonymously if preferred.

Share what you have learned about confession with other church or group leaders and encourage them to lead their own groups toward regular, thorough, biblical confession.

Pray for the people in your groups, churches, and across your city, to embrace confession as a central discipline of their spiritual lives.

In this chapter we learned that the Things Above include not only those elements we can see in our picture, but also truths about us, such as that we are blameless before God in Christ. What other truths can we learn from Scripture concerning our *condition* in Christ?

Chapter 5

Living in Union With Jesus

*But I say, walk by the Spirit, and you
will not carry out the desire of the
flesh. Galatians 5:16*

In the last chapter, we began looking at our individual relationship with Jesus as one of the Things Above. However, to be precise, we did not look at our relationship with Jesus so much as the righteous standing we have before God, thanks to Him. We saw that He gave us right standing by removing unrighteousness from us through His blood, and that He means to apply His blood to us here, cleansing us when we confess sins. When we receive cleansing, our tendency to repeat similar sins decreases because we don't have the pressure of unrighteousness working against us.

However, we can confess all our sins and develop a good discipline of regular confession, yet still have a difficult time overcoming certain sins. We may find ourselves defeated time and again even despite our cleansing. It is frustrating but there is a reason for it. Cleansing gets our foot off the brakes in our pursuit of righteousness, but it doesn't get our foot on the gas pedal because it only removes residual unrighteousness. It does not provide positive power for righteous living so that we can overcome sin. Cleansing's limitation is that it does not deal with our sin nature, which is always at work against us. We need something else to deal with that, something that will get our foot on the gas and provide power for holy and righteous living.

The Nature of Our Relationship with Jesus

We find it when we look carefully at our individual relationship with Jesus Himself. Remember that when Jesus joined us to Himself to take us through His cross and grave and resurrection and ascension, He didn't just bring us along on a journey as one might bring a suitcase. Nor did he bring us along as companions to have with Him along the way and to be with Him at the end. No, He *joined* Himself to us, and that means we have a spirit-level connection with Him that is permanent and can be potent in our lives. Recall what He asked of the Father:

> *I do not ask on behalf of these alone, but for those also who believe in Me through their word; that they may all be one; even as You, Father, are in Me and I in You, that they also may be in Us, so that the world may believe that You sent Me.*
> **John 17:20-21**

The relationship that Jesus had in mind was for us to be as closely related to Him as He and the Father are to each other. And that is exactly what He accomplished. Our spirits are now intimately connected to Jesus, so much so that the Scriptures seem to have difficulty describing our exact relationship. We see it portrayed two ways. We are told we are with Him.

> *...having been buried with Him in baptism, in which you were also raised up with Him through faith in the working of God, who raised Him from the dead. When you were dead in your transgressions and the uncircumcision of your flesh, He made you alive together with Him, having forgiven us all our transgressions*
> **Colossians 2:12-13**

> *...and [God] raised us up with Him, and seated us with Him in the heavenly places...*
> **Ephesians 2:6**

And we are told that we are in Him.

> *But by [God's] doing you are in Christ Jesus, who became to us wisdom from God, and righteousness and sanctification, and redemption.*
> **1 Corinthians 1:30**

> *Now He who establishes us with you in Christ and anointed us is God.*
> **2 Corinthians 1:21**

> *Therefore if anyone is in Christ, he is a new creature; the old things passed away; behold, new things have come.*
> **2 Corinthians 5:17**

> *Blessed be the God and Father of our Lord Jesus Christ, who has blessed us with every spiritual blessing in the heavenly places in Christ.*
> **Ephesians 1:3**

But passages describing us as being in Christ vastly outnumber passages that say we are with Christ, so the emphasis is far more indicative of an intimate relationship than merely a close association. When we look back at our picture of the things above, we can see that it is not quite as precise as we would like. Our picture makes it look like there is some distance between us and Jesus, and in that regard it falls short of the truth. That's why there are also arrows. They represent the Holy Spirit, Who is one with Jesus in the Trinity, and is within all believers as well, since all of us have received the Holy Spirit from Him.[10]

> *Or do you not know that your body is a temple of the Holy Spirit who is in you, whom you have from God, and that you are not your own?*
> **1 Corinthians 6:19**

So our picture isn't perfect, and probably can't be, but we can trust the Scriptures that we have a deeply intimate, personal relationship and spirit-level connection with Jesus through His Holy Spirit. Jesus was willing to go to any length to achieve it, including uniting Himself with us while we were still sinners in rebellion against God.

> *But God demonstrates His own love toward us, in that while we were yet sinners, Christ died for us.*
> **Romans 5:8**

In truth it was not just our sins He took on the cross. He took each of us in our entirety as individuals. This means that He took us with our good qualities like our creativity, preferences, and personalities. And He took us with our bad qualities like our rebellion, wickedness, ingratitude, and our record of sins. The things that derived from sin died with Him on the cross; he redeemed the rest. He also gave us life in Himself to make us complete in Him.

> *And in Him you have been made complete, and He is the head over all rule and authority*
> **Colossians 2:10**

---

[10] The Holy Spirit is so intimately connected with Jesus that He is sometimes even called the Spirit of Jesus Christ, the Spirit of His Son, or the Spirit of Christ. See Philippians 1:19, Galatians 4:6, and 1 Peter 1:11, respectively.

When He was raised, He brought us with Him as an inheritance, a hard won treasure and a precious possession, forever made holy and intimately close to Him by the power of God.

> *I pray that the eyes of your heart may be enlightened, so that you will know what is the hope of His calling, what are the riches of the glory of His inheritance in the saints*
> **Ephesians 1:18**

When we contemplate the work that He did to obtain us as His people, how costly and extravagant His sacrifice was, and how willingly He underwent this, we can know with certainty that He must also have some great purpose for us. The Kingdom Way teaches us that our heavenly connection with Jesus is meant to have an outworking on earth, and given the astounding supernatural character of our union with Jesus, we should expect something big. What is it?

It is the power of His life working in and through us on earth as it works in us in heaven. Jesus made us like Himself in the heavens, in the sense of being holy, sanctified, and righteous. Therefore, we can fully expect Him to be about making us holy, sanctified, and righteous on earth through His great power and the intimate relationship we share. How that comes about is the subject of this chapter.

Our Death and Resurrection with Jesus

To explore how His power can give us victory over sin, we're going to have to backtrack and take a closer look at the narrative we established in Chapter one, where we saw that all the things that happened to Jesus happened to us through Him as well. Our journey with Jesus encompasses our crucifixion and burial with Him, as well as our resurrection with Him. We'll take a moment to look at these ideas a bit more closely. In the following verses, Paul is quite clear about our union with Jesus in His crucifixion and burial.

> *Or don't you know that all of us who were baptized[11] into*

---

[11] As elsewhere, baptism here also means union with Jesus in His death and resurrection. Paul is saying that our connection with Jesus includes our union with Him in His death and burial, in effect, saying "don't you know that all of us who were joined in union with Jesus were joined in union with Him in

Christ Jesus were baptized into his death? We were therefore buried with him through baptism into death.
Romans 6:3-4a

Elsewhere, Paul similarly asserts…

In Him you were also circumcised with a circumcision made without hands, in the removal of the body of the flesh by the circumcision of Christ; having been buried with Him in baptism, in which you were also raised up with Him through faith in the working of God, who raised Him from the dead.
Colossians 2:11-12

And…

For you have died...
Colossians 3:3a

And this death occurred through Jesus' crucifixion:

I have been crucified with Christ.
Galatians 2:20a

Paul teaches that when Jesus died, we were intimately connected with Him to the point of dying with Him. Fortunately, Paul gets more specific about exactly what died with Jesus, since obviously our pulse didn't stop and our bodies weren't put in a grave.

For we know that our old self was crucified with him so that the body ruled by sin might be done away with, that we should no longer be slaves to sin— because anyone who has died has been set free from sin.
Romans 6:6-7

His death? We were therefore buried with Him through our union with Him in death." See the footnote in Chapter One for our previous discussion of this usage.

Those who belong to Christ Jesus have crucified the flesh with its passions and desires.
Galatians 5:24

It was our old self that was crucified with Christ and died with Him. What is this old self? It was our slavery to a sinful nature. Just as Peter says:

He Himself bore our sins in His body on the cross, so that we might die to sin and live to righteousness; for by His wounds you were healed.
1 Peter 2:24

So, the death that we underwent with Jesus was the death of our sinful nature. This means that, as hard as it is to imagine, we are under no obligation to sin any more. Our sinful nature *has been killed*. Although we still have a tendency to believe that sinning is inevitable, the Scriptures are quite clear about this point.

Therefore if anyone is in Christ, he is a new creature; the old things passed away; behold, new things have come.
2 Corinthians 5:17

We are new creations and our old self is gone. It passed away on the cross with Jesus. We have a new life that is connected with Jesus because we were raised with Him:

...and your life is hidden with Christ in God.
Colossians 3:3b

This new life is intimately and permanently connected with Jesus. Our old life, in which we were stuck sinning and couldn't stop, is done. It need no longer have power over us because *a death occurred that counts for us as the death of that old self.* We now have a new nature of being alive to God through Jesus. Our new life is the living relationship we have with Him in the heavens where we are forever joined to Him and are in Him.

Some years back, I looked at this teaching as most people do and considered it hard to understand. Underlying that was a wish to know how it could be true that I was dead to sin and alive to God when sin seemed so inevitable for me. I struggled with it, thinking that if I could just master the technicalities of *how* God did all this I would be able to take a leap forward and have victory over sin in my life. I didn't realize that trying to understand *how* was a waste of time and a hindrance. It is a miracle, just like the rest of our journey with Jesus, and therefore, it fundamentally defies explanation.[12]

But this teaching comes from the Word of God, and we've studied some things about that already. We remember what the Kingdom Way teaches us about God's Word – that it must go forth with prayer to become an increasingly settled matter within us. So lay aside any tendency in your heart to stand above His Word, doubting rather than accepting it. Confess and obtain cleansing for all such sins. Pray through these passages regularly, asking that He would take away doubt and that His Word would go deep into you, becoming a settled matter of belief. Just as Paul commends the Thessalonians, let us also have the same attitude they did.

> *For this reason we also constantly thank God that when you received the Word of God which you heard from us, you accepted it not as the word of men, but for what it really is, the Word of God, which also performs its work in you who believe.*
> **1 Thessalonians 2:13**

And we will press on to see how God brings us the benefits of all we've seen so far.

---

[12] However, even if it is fruitless to insist we understand *how* it happened, there is no reason we can't look for evidence *that* it happened. For some the experience of reckoning with God as King and Father can be viewed as evidence of this death. Such an encounter can be a painful and terrible moment of humbling accompanied by anguish of soul. Some people flee from this encounter as from death, never to be saved, while others follow through and afterward experience what they can only describe as new life. While not every believer's experience at salvation follows this pattern, most Christians are aware of other believers who have experienced it, and all of us should periodically experience something like this as we walk with God, since this is part of dying to self.

Living in Union with Jesus

The Kingdom Way teaches us to set our minds on the Things Above, and in this case that includes the journey we took with Jesus. The Scriptures are clear that we died to sin and are alive to Christ. These are central facts that form the basis for overcoming sin. It is not surprising that when Paul laid out these truths in Romans 6:1-10 that the next thing was a command to set our minds on them.

> *Even so consider yourselves to be dead to sin, but alive to God in Christ Jesus*
> **Romans 6:11**

In fact, this is the very first command in all of Romans. We are to consider that we are dead to sin and alive to God in Jesus Christ. This is something we decide to do. We must make the decision to set our minds on this as true, which means we bank on the words of Scripture rather than what our natural thoughts insist is true. This is the first obstacle to overcome on the way to living a life that is powered by our intimate connection with Jesus.

It is common for us to look at our lives and see all kinds of "evidence" to the contrary when it comes to seeing ourselves as free from the power of sin. But when we look to our own histories and habits to tell us what is true about ourselves, we are not setting our minds on the Things Above. We are setting them on earthly things, namely our own lives and stories. Paul commands us to set our minds on a different story, one in which Jesus did a miracle for us by providing a death and resurrection for us. His work changes the truth about the deepest places within us.

Set your mind on this: You are dead to sin and alive to God in Christ Jesus. Let this become a grounding truth in your thoughts and outlook. To set your mind on these things, to consider yourself dead and alive, as we're taught, is God's will for you on earth based on the things in heaven. They are Things Above; faith-based obedience will consider them to be true. Take hope in this truth because it is one of the great and precious promises to which Peter refers, just as we've seen.

> *His divine power has given us everything we need for a godly life through our knowledge of him who called us by*

his own glory and goodness. Through these he has given us
his very great and precious promises, so that through them
you may participate in the divine nature, having escaped
the corruption in the world caused by evil desires.
2 Peter 1:3-4

The promises Peter writes about allow us to *participate in the divine*
nature – that is, experience a powerful life, intimately connected to
Jesus – *having escaped the corruption...caused by evil desires.* This
denotes our escape from slavery to sin and is perfectly consistent with
Paul's teaching.

But the Kingdom Way always includes prayer, and where living out
our union with Jesus is concerned, things are no different. For these
truths to go forth in us requires prayer and devotion to His Word, as
well as faith-based obedience to set our minds on them. Our prayer is
that the truth of these passages would go down into us and become a
settled matter of confident belief.

Paul does not stop there. It is good to know that we are no longer
slaves to sin and are alive to God in Jesus. It is important to settle on
this as a grounding truth in our lives. But it does not provide us with an
understanding of how we live in our union with Jesus, which is where
we finally get our foot on the gas pedal. Believing that we are dead to
sin and alive to God is the equivalent of finding out that there is such a
thing as a gas pedal. Next, we find out how to get our foot on it and get
moving. In the following verses Paul says:

Therefore do not let sin reign in your mortal body so that
you obey its lusts, and do not go on presenting the members
of your body to sin as instruments of unrighteousness; but
present yourselves to God as those alive from the dead, and
your members as instruments of righteousness to God.
Romans 6:12-13

The command here is to *present yourselves to God as those alive from*
the dead, and your members as instruments of righteousness to God.
The only way to obey this command is by prayer. There are two things
we present to God: ourselves, which includes our minds, our will and
all else we think of as ourselves; and the members of our bodies,

which includes our body parts and the various abilities we have through them.

For me, obeying this command often sounds something like this. "Father, your Word says I am dead to sin and alive to you in Jesus. I present myself to you in the light of this truth, as one that is dead to sin and alive to you. Live your perfect life through me. I present my mind to you for your use, that your thoughts should be mine. I present my eyes to you that they should be instruments of your use, set apart for your holy purposes. I present my mouth, my tongue, my words to you, that they speak only what is good and pure, that which comes from you." Usually my prayer goes on in specifics like this because I find it helpful to make sure I've presented my whole self to Him, and have not held anything back.

This is a prayer in which we are essentially saying to God that we surrender to our union with Jesus, so that by His holiness we can live holy, by His righteousness we can live righteous, by His wisdom we can live wisely, and so on. But it is also a statement of faith in God, that we are ready to wait expectantly for Him to answer this prayer though Jesus. He is just as ready to live in union with us here as He is in the heavens.

When we pray like this, and draw near to Jesus with the expectation that He will draw near to us, we find that is exactly what He does, bringing with Him peace beyond measure, joy inexpressible, companionship, victory over sin, quiet power to minister to others, wisdom and insight, and compassion for things that are near to His heart. Living in union with Jesus is abundant life that wells up and spills over, so much more than we can muster up on our own. It is the life we want, the life He means for us to have.

What I am describing has been called abiding in Christ, walking by the Spirit, being filled with the Spirit, putting on the new self and several other terms that take in various aspects of it. Abiding has been written about extensively by other authors for generations, most notably by Andrew Murray in his classic book *Abiding in Christ*. I find that abiding in Christ is the term I most commonly use to refer to this. I think it is a good one because abiding denotes rest rather than effort, and that is one of the most beautiful aspects of it. Several authors have defined abiding in different ways, and I will as well.

Abiding in Christ is living in our union with Jesus with expectant faith that permits Him to be and do, in and through us, all that we typically strive or desire to be and do for Him, but cannot.

There is a lot in that definition so let me take it apart piece by piece. First, we *live in our union with Jesus*. We know that the Things Above are meant to have an impact here on earth. Jesus brought us through a death that suffices as the conquering of sin in our lives. He then took us into heaven with Him where we have an intimate spirit-level connection to Him. Through abiding in Christ, He provides the means to live out this spirit-level union with Him in our daily lives.

Second, we live in that union *with expectant faith*. Expectant faith banks on Jesus doing what He says He will do. It is essentially confident, expectant waiting on Jesus, and is directly linked to the fact that we are setting our minds on Him as one of the Things Above. In this case our expectation is that He *will* come into our lives in the moment and make the kind of difference only He can make. We expect that our union with Him will bear fruit because Jesus is faithful to His promises.

We express expectant faith by going to Him in prayer. The Kingdom Way shows us that prayer is essential. We present ourselves to God in prayer as people dead to sin and alive to God in Christ. We present the members of our bodies to Him as instruments of righteousness, to be used by Him.

Third, our expectant faith *permits Jesus* to come and fulfill the kind of relationship and power in us here that He has already established for us by bringing us into the heavens with Him. Without prayer and expectant faith, we bar the doors of our heart from the inside. We deny Him the opportunity to fill us with His Holy Spirit. However, through prayer accompanied by faith we throw open the doors of our heart and eagerly await Him.

Fourth, He comes *to be and do, certain things in and through us*. He comes to *be certain things within us*, such as righteousness, life, and love. He comes to *be certain things through us*, like the fragrance of Himself to those around us. He comes to *do certain things in us,* such as sanctify us and keep us from stumbling. And He comes to *do certain things through us,* such as heal, preach, encourage, exhort and do miracles. You can think of this part of the definition like this:

Jesus Wants to…

	…In Us	…Through Us
Be…	**Be in us:** Righteousness, Wisdom, Sanctification, Redemption (I Cor 1:30) Life (Col 3:4) Love (1 John 4:9, 12)	**Be through us:** The fragrance of Christ (2 Cor 2:15)
Do…	**Do in us:** Renew our minds (Rom 12:2, Eph 4:23) Sanctify us (Heb 2:11) Keep us from stumbling (Jude 24)	**Do through us:** Heal (Acts 3:6-7) Deliver from Demons (Acts 16:18) Preach (Rom 15:18-19, 2 Cor 5:20) Encourage (Phil 2:1-2) Exhort (1 Thess 4:1) Raise the dead, Etc. (Matt 10:8)

Fifth, the things He brings are those *we typically strive or desire to be or do, but cannot.* We constantly tend to do things on our own, in our own strength. We try to be righteous on our own. We try to be spiritually influential to others on our own. We try to wrangle our minds into conformance with God's will on our own. And we try to do our works in our own power. We fail at all these things when we leave out Jesus.

When we abide in Him, Jesus provides all that we lack for all of these things and more. He has joined Himself to us, and through His Holy Spirit He is in us, so that all these areas of our lives and ministries can see power that is far beyond what we can bring to the table on our own. However, if we are merely reliant on our own strength for these things, we will not see the power of God at work. We will get what we can bring to the table and nothing more.

Which brings us back around to Paul's teaching on this: we are commanded to consider ourselves dead to sin and alive to God in Jesus. We are commanded to present ourselves to Him as those alive from the dead, and to present the members of our bodies as instruments of service to Him. When we disobey these commands and do not go to Him, we are left to our own power, and the results are of merely human measure, lacking divine power. When we wing it like this, we may look like we've pulled it off in the eyes of others. We might look like we've succeeded at preaching, or being righteous, but the power of the Holy Spirit that accomplishes the purposes of God will be absent. Our neglect of surrender to Jesus relegates Him to the sideline. We miss out seeing what God can do, and instead we get only what we can do.

But there is even more to abiding in Christ and walking by the Spirit. What I have described so far is available to us because the Holy Spirit of Jesus is *in us* and means to be working these things in and through us. But we are also *in Him*, and there are things to be gained from that aspect of our union as well. Just as Jesus says, abiding is a two way relationship, He in us, and we in Him:

> *Abide in Me, and I in you. As the branch cannot bear fruit of itself unless it abides in the vine, so neither can you unless you abide in Me.*
> **John 15:4**

And here are some things we find in Christ: peace (John 14:27), rest (Matt 11:28-29) and welcome (Acts 10:35). We obtain these things in the same way, by abiding in Him.

The result of all this is empowerment by Jesus to be and do what He desires. Abiding is His means of providing power over sin, of ministering to others through us, and of bringing us into joy and fellowship with Him. Abiding in Christ gets our foot on the gas[13], and

---

[13] Confession is important, and is rightly the first spiritual discipline new believers should learn. However, abiding in Christ *is the heart of Christian life*. Just because confession comes first in our development doesn't mean it should forever precede abiding. As we learn to walk with Jesus, we should always see abiding as the first place we go in our spiritual life. Jesus Himself is our life. When we go to Him first, everything else becomes easier,

it really works. He is ready at all times to meet us through abiding and be the power we need to enliven us for fruitfulness and abundant life.

Abiding as Seen in the Scriptures

We can see the principles of abiding in many Scriptures. Jesus spoke several times about His walk with God and the manner in which He lived and worked. What He said makes sense only when we recognize that He abided in the Father.

> *So Jesus said, "When you lift up the Son of Man, then you will know that I am He, and I do nothing on My own initiative, but I speak these things as the Father taught Me. And He who sent Me is with Me; He has not left Me alone, for I always do the things that are pleasing to Him."*
> **John 8:28-29**

In these verses Jesus says He does nothing on His own initiative. In His union with the Father He was surrendered to the point of having given His work over to God entirely.

Similarly, it was through abiding that Jesus did miracles.

> *"If I do not do the works of My Father, do not believe Me; but if I do them, though you do not believe Me, believe the works, so that you may know and understand that the Father is in Me, and I in the Father."*
> **John 10:37-38**

Here, Jesus explains that He did His miraculous works through unity with the Father. His statement about being in the Father, and the Father being in Him, is the same kind of statement we should be able to make about our relationship with Jesus. If that sounds extreme, remember

---

including confession. We should abide while using His Word, telling of the Kingdom, confessing sins, and all the other things we will discuss in coming chapters.

The truth is, even when one foot is on the brakes, the gas pedal still works quite well and will move us forward! We don't *have to* get our foot off the brakes by confessing sins, but we will want to, and we will go farther faster when we do. Abiding in Christ is primary.

that the Things Above came to be in answer to Jesus' prayer. He asked
for that level of unity with Him to be the case for us as well. We
shouldn't be shocked or surprised that He would be willing to join
Himself to us so completely here on earth when He has already done
so in the heavens.

Our chief concern is the level of surrender we bring to Him.
Fortunately, a surrendered heart is something that He can develop in us
over time, given the opportunity. We must begin there. If we are
faithful with a little, He will give us more over time.

Later, in explaining how the Father could be known through Him,
Jesus said

> *Do you not believe that I am in the Father, and the Father
> is in Me? The words that I say to you I do not speak on My
> own initiative, but the Father abiding in Me does His
> works. Believe Me that I am in the Father and the Father is
> in Me; otherwise believe because of the works themselves.*
> **John 14:10-11**

Jesus was able to do miracles and speak and minister with power and
wisdom because He was abiding in the Father and the Father was
abiding in Him. We often think that Jesus could do miracles because
He was divine, because He brought His own power to bear to do the
things He did. This is not the case. Jesus gave up His divine attributes
and lived as a man, just as Paul makes clear in Philippians 2:5-7. He
could have grasped the power He had through the Godhead, but didn't,
instead emptying Himself of all that and relying on the Father.

This provides helpful perspective for us. Since Jesus did miracles
through abiding in the Father, and has given us the ability to abide in
Him through the same sort of union He has with the Father (c.f. John
17:21-22), then we should do the same things He did. And that is what
He says in the next verse.

> *Truly, truly, I say to you, he who believes in Me, the works
> that I do, he will do also; and greater works than these he
> will do; because I go to the Father.*
> **John 14:12**

Paul also speaks in the same way about his own life and power for ministry.

> *For this purpose also I labor, striving according to His power, which mightily works within me.*
> **Colossians 1:29**

> *I can do all things through Him who strengthens me.*
> **Philippians 4:13**

Paul also gives us glimpses of abiding when he discusses his ministry and the source of his power.

> *Now we have received, not the spirit of the world, but the Spirit who is from God, so that we may know the things freely given to us by God, which things we also speak, not in words taught by human wisdom, but in those taught by the Spirit, combining spiritual thoughts with spiritual words.*
> **I Corinthians 2:12-13**

Paul is describing the process of abiding, in which the Holy Spirit guides both the thoughts and words he should speak. He also describes how the life of Jesus is manifested in him and his companions through their sufferings.

> *But we have this treasure in earthen vessels, so that the surpassing greatness of the power will be of God and not from ourselves; we are afflicted in every way, but not crushed; perplexed, but not despairing; persecuted, but not forsaken; struck down, but not destroyed; always carrying about in the body the dying of Jesus, so that the life of Jesus also may be manifested in our body. For we who live are constantly being delivered over to death for Jesus' sake, so that the life of Jesus also may be manifested in our mortal flesh.*
> **1 Corinthians 4:7-11**

To Paul, the fact that trials are insufficient to break or discourage them is evidence of the powerful life that works within them. It is the life of

Jesus that comes through abiding. In another passage Paul describes how God perfects His power through our weakness.[14]

> *And He has said to me, "My grace is sufficient for you, for power is perfected in weakness." Most gladly, therefore, I will rather boast about my weaknesses, so that the power of Christ may dwell in me.*
> **2 Corinthians 12:9**

Peter also speaks of abiding as the means by which God receives glory through Jesus.

> *Whoever speaks, is to do so as one who is speaking the utterances of God; whoever serves is to do so as one who is serving by the strength which God supplies; so that in all things God may be glorified through Jesus Christ, to whom belongs the glory and dominion forever and ever. Amen.*
> **1 Peter 4:11**

And in Hebrews, the writer's prayer is that through Jesus, God will equip the readers with the very things that come by abiding in Christ.

> *Now the God of peace, who brought up from the dead the great Shepherd of the sheep through the blood of the eternal covenant, even Jesus our Lord, equip you in every good thing to do His will, working in us that which is pleasing in His sight, through Jesus Christ, to whom be the*

---

[14] Not that we are purposefully to *be weak*. That is passivity and is contrary to the gifts and abilities God has given us. Rather, we are to be reliant in the areas in which we *are weak*. Our areas of weakness are numerous and include, among other things, our inability to overcome sin on our own, our inability to bring the power of God on our own, our need for wisdom, and our inability to victoriously overcome natural reactions to suffering. We are not to passively lie around waiting for God to do what He has given us some ability to do. But we are similarly not to do the things that we can do without also relying on God to provide the power, wisdom, strength, etc. that make our efforts fruitful. Taken the right way, the old adage "let go and let God" is a good description of abiding. Taken the wrong way, it prescribes sinful passivity and fecklessness. Jesus and Paul were not passive people, but they were reliant on God.

glory forever and ever. Amen.
Hebrews 13:20-21

Most of the language we see about walking by the Spirit, living in Christ, being transformed in our minds, being renewed in the spirit of our minds, and being filled with the Holy Spirit refers to abiding in Christ.

Abiding and Surrender

The wonderful qualities of Jesus are available to us through prayer, surrender, and fellowship with Him in the Holy Spirit. But to fully enumerate the benefits of abiding in Christ is as impossible as it is to fully describe Jesus as a person. Part of the Christian life is to grow in our ability to experience Him more deeply. This is something He is eager to lead us into over time.

Through abiding, Jesus will always answer our prayers of surrender and will meet us with everything He can. But for those areas in which we are not surrendered, He will not be able to meet us, because in those things we are still self sufficient, or even resistant to Him.

Say I am tempted to make an angry outburst at work, but instead I call upon Jesus and rely on His power to resist and overcome anger. I would be surrendering myself to Him. In such a case He will certainly come and be all I need in that moment. He will never, ever fail me because He can't fail.

But suppose I also steal little things from work and think nothing of it. I may find Him present to overcome my anger, but He won't be able to do anything about my thieving heart because I have not surrendered it to Him. He will likely be trying to get my attention about thievery, but as long as I resist Him, He will be shut out from helping me overcome in that area. He will not compel my surrender because the Father has given us authority over our choices. So abiding coincides with surrender, but will not extend beyond our surrender. It is no help for areas in which we are determined to sin.

Jesus is also aware of our sincerity. He knows the difference between surrender and manipulation and will never bend to our will. The problem comes when we have not perceived we are trying to manipulate Him. We will find that He doesn't respond the way we want. If we want Him to give us power to heal someone, but we want it so that we can receive the glory, He will most often not grant the healing. We may even think that He is unfaithful when in fact it is we who are calling upon Him with selfish motives. We are making as if to call upon Him, but primarily we want Him to serve our interests. Like doubt, this is a form of double-mindedness.

> *For that man ought not to expect that he will receive anything from the Lord, being a double-minded man, unstable in all his ways.*
> **James 1:7-8**

Such double-mindedness is all too common in our hearts, and can show up in things far more subtle than asking for healing. We easily deceive ourselves about our motives. So when we call upon Jesus, it is Jesus Whom we must welcome in our hearts. We must give glory to Him, something that often comes at the cost of giving up our own desires. This is the surrender He requires.

That being said, Jesus is generous with His grace. Abiding is a blessing freely given, one that He wants for us enough to have died for each of us to have it. He is not harsh, nor does He withhold Himself in a stingy manner, waiting for us to perfect ourselves. It is He that means to perfect us by abiding in us. He welcomes us to abide in Him for just that reason. The cautionary notes above are meant to keep us from drifting into misunderstanding, not to paint a picture of Jesus that is other than abundantly gracious. Let this be clear: Jesus wants nearness to you and has gone to great lengths to have it. Surrender to Him as best you can and He will always meet you there, and you will find that you have all you need for life and Godliness in Him. He will also lead you deeper. There is no limit to the depths to which He can take you because abiding can be as big as He is.

Prayer in Jesus' Name

Another quick glance at the Things Above shows us that we are in union with Jesus *and He is praying*. You should be good enough at this by now to see the Kingdom Way here: however Jesus is praying in heaven, God wants us to be praying the same way here. Since the intimate connection we have with Jesus works out as abiding, it makes sense that there should be a relationship between abiding and prayer. Let us look at this more closely.

In John 14:10-11, Jesus explains how all He does is rooted in His abiding relationship with the Father. He then encourages the disciples by saying they will do even greater things precisely because He is going to the Father (v.12.) Jesus is looking ahead, speaking about a time when He will be in heaven and we will abide in Him on earth. Verses 10-12 are about abiding, and the following two verses tie directly into abiding as well.

> *Whatever you ask in My name, that will I do, so that the Father may be glorified in the Son. If you ask Me anything in My name, I will do it.*
> **John 14:13-14**

In this verse, the promise about answered prayer is linked to the phrase *in My name*. That's what we'll connect with abiding as we go on.

And since His Word is central to the Kingdom Way, it is not surprising there is a connection between His Word and answered prayer.

> *If you abide in Me, and My words abide in you, ask whatever you wish, and it will be done for you.*
> **John 15:7**

This should remind us of His Word becoming a settled matter in us.

The subject of prayer comes up again in John 16:23b-28. It is a long passage containing several elements of interest to us.

> *"Truly, truly, I say to you, if you ask the Father for anything in My name, He will give it to you. Until now you have asked for nothing in My name; ask and you will receive, so that your joy may be made full."*
> **John 16:23-24**

Jesus again promises that when we pray *in His name* the Father will give us what we ask for. What is praying in Jesus' name? It has traditionally been understood as praying as He would pray, in the sense of asking for the kind of things He would ask for. Yet we have all had the experience of asking for such things without receiving them. Why does this happen? [15]

On closer examination, praying in Jesus' name also means praying *like* Jesus would pray, that is, with the same heart and attitude that He would have. Jesus' heart was obedient to the will of the Father. I mentioned this above when I discussed having a desire to heal people from pure motives rather than selfish ones. Similarly, if I am praying for my Sunday school class, asking for God's Word to go forth, but my heart's reason for this is so people will look at me as a good teacher, I am asking for something Jesus wants to do but I am not asking for it the way He would ask for it. I am not praying in Jesus' name because I am asking in self-interest, something Jesus never did.

God wants us to pray for His Word to go forth, for people to be healed, and for all kinds of other good things. But if there are sinful attitudes within us, the first thing He usually tries to do is root them out and obtain repentance in us. In my own life, I find there are often numerous things He wants to deal with inside me before I can truly pray in Jesus' name. However, we often rush on to our next request and give Him little chance to address these things. Our prayers go unanswered as a result.

Allowing God to speak to those things within us that He wants to address takes time. If we give Him time, He will often bring Scriptures to mind. He can do this in many ways, but in the context of prayer one of the ways He does this is directly through the prompting of the Holy Spirit within us. Paying attention to our consciences during this process is important, as there may be things we need to confess. However, if we're not abiding in Christ while we pray, we will probably miss what He is trying to do in us. When He does get our attention it is usually with the goal that His Words will go forth in us. Recall what Jesus said:

---

[15] Prayers go unanswered for many reasons. A full discussion of them is beyond the scope of this book. The following is a partial list. We are not persistent (Luke 18:1-8); our sins hinder our prayers (1 Peter 3:7); spiritual forces of darkness are interfering Daniel 10:12-13; or heart attitudes within others are closed to God (Matthew 13:58).

If you abide in Me, and My words abide in you, ask whatever you wish, and it will be done for you.
John 15:7

He is looking for His Words to become a settled matter, for them to abide in us. This is one of the conditions He gave us for having prayers answered. When we do receive His Words and settle on them, His will is being done and we get a step closer to praying our original request like Jesus would. We want to reach the point where we are asking *what* He would ask, and asking it *as* He would ask it.

Abiding in Christ and His Word abiding in us are essential to answered prayer. Both are required. But there is another aspect to this as well. We've noted that Jesus is praying in the heavens, and we want to connect with Him in His prayers through abiding. Speaking from my own experience, it seems that when we are abiding in Christ, and are in prayer for things that are in keeping with God's will, that Jesus shares His prayers with us as a means of guiding us. Note the following verses:

These things I have spoken to you in figurative language; an hour is coming when I will no longer speak to you in figurative language, but will tell you plainly of the Father. In that day you will ask in My name, and I do not say to you that I will request of the Father on your behalf;
John 16:25-26

Jesus will be plain with us about the Father. One of the things Jesus will be clear about is our heart's condition before the Him. He wants us to be able to work through heart issues with the Father so that we can pray unhindered and receive what we ask for. When Jesus gets us to this place of surrender, He obtains a rare thing on the earth – someone that is able to bring to the Father prayers in union with Himself, so that the prayers come from Jesus and us together through that union.

When I pray for my class the same thing Jesus is praying for them, *and* I do so with the same heart Jesus has, Jesus and I are unified in our prayers; we are praying together in unity. We are both making the same request to God. Jesus doesn't ask the Father *on our behalf*, as though we have limited access to the Father. Rather, at that point our prayers have the sweet aroma of the Son praying through us as we also pray to the Father. At this point, Jesus welcomes us into His prayers, and finds us willing and able to bring them to God with Him, in the same heart, the same Spirit.

This is what it means to pray in Jesus' name, and it is intimately tied to abiding and the extent to which God's Word is settled in our hearts. It is only by abiding that we can reach the place of harmony and unity with Jesus that permits our prayers to be to the Father as Jesus' own. When we pray this way, we have synchronized our prayers with Jesus' own prayers. From the Father's perspective, He is hearing the same prayer from Jesus in heaven, and from us on earth. He is, so to speak, getting it in both ears at the same time, in the most pleasing way, and it is such prayers that He holds in high regard.

Conclusion

We are commanded to abide because Jesus wants the world to know He came from the Father and is the Savior of the world. He has provided everything we need to live the godly and fruitful life He means for us, and to minister with power, grace, and love through Him. Therefore let us be reminded of Peter's promise to us,

> *His divine power has granted to us everything pertaining to life and godliness, through the true knowledge of Him who called us by His own glory and excellence. For by these He has granted to us His precious and magnificent promises, so that by them you may become partakers of the divine nature, having escaped the corruption that is in the world by lust.*
> **2 Peter 1:3-4**

and obey Paul's command,

> *But I say, walk by the Spirit, and you will not carry out the desire of the flesh.*
> **Galatians 5:16**

so that the world will know that Jesus came from the Father.

Challenges

Begin considering yourself dead to sin and alive to God in Christ. This requires meditation upon, and acceptance of the Things Above. If this is difficult, you may need to pray for God's Word to go forth in you, something that will be helped by memorizing verses that teach these things. Be alert to the danger of focusing on the supposed overwhelming power of your sin. To focus on that is to take your eyes of the Things Above, namely Jesus, through whom we did indeed die to sin. Set your mind on the Things Above.

Present yourself to God in prayer as one alive from the dead. Present the parts of your body to Him in prayer as instruments of righteousness. If you find it helpful, use the prayer I use, provided above.

Read the Gospel of John, noting Jesus' statements about His walk with God, specifically how He credits the works He does to the Father. Compare each of these passages to Philippians 2:5-7, which tells us that Jesus did not work through His divine nature but rather as a man. What can you learn about abiding in Christ from the way Jesus abides in the Father?

In John 15:7 Jesus says, "If you abide in Me, and My words abide in you, ask whatever you wish, and it will be done for you." In light of this verse and Chapter Two, how important is it for God's Word to become a settled matter for us? What relationship is there between our maturity in God's Word and answered prayer in our lives?

Consider Jesus' prayer in John 17, the one we have been studying. This was an extremely large request to the Father, yet it began to be answered within about twelve hours. What does this tell us about the place of God's Word within Jesus?

Find Andrew Murray's book *Abiding in Christ*. It is a daily devotional set up for a month. Use these devotionals at your own pace, reading and rereading each one until you begin to experience Jesus in the ways described. If you have especial difficulty grasping a particular concept move on to the next one. It is a deep, rich book with a wealth of material to help your growth. On my first reading, I found it took me three to five days to digest a single day's devotional. After twenty-five years, I still return to this masterpiece.

Make abiding in Christ the primary objective of your devotional times and *all* Bible study times. This means slowing down to spend time with God while you are in His Word.

Practice abiding while praying. Take time over one thing that is on your mind to request from God. Let God lead you as you consider this thing. Search the Scriptures to see what God's will is likely to be about the concern. Allow the Holy Spirit to point out selfish or unbiblical motives in your desire for this. Allow Him to purify your motives and desires. Seek Jesus as the one Who is near, for His wisdom in the matter. Ask Him to let you hear how He is praying. Your desire is to make your requests in Jesus' name. Don't be surprised if He works on you rather extensively in this process. He is trying to bring you to the point that you *can* make your request in His name. Your fellowship is important to Him throughout this process. He paid dearly to obtain it.

Answer these questions: who sustains you in your union with Jesus in the heavens, you or Jesus? If God's will is done on earth as in heaven, who will sustain you in your union with Jesus on earth, you or Jesus?

Assess your perspective on Jesus' promises about answered prayer. Do you feel more receptive to the idea that He will answer your prayers when you abide in Him, or when His Word abides in you? Are you resistant to one or other principle? Ask God to show you why you are less receptive to one or the other, and take steps to improve in that area using all the tools of repentance we have studied.

Chapter 6

Unity in the Church

We ought always to give thanks to God for you, brethren, as is only fitting, because your faith is greatly enlarged, and the love of each one of you toward one another grows ever greater. 1 Thessalonians 1:3

In the last chapter, we looked at our individual relationship with Jesus and learned that, through it, we can abide in Christ, be renewed within, and become empowered for service through Him. In this chapter we will broaden our scope and study the relationship we all have with each other and Jesus. We can picture it like this:

We can see that we are joined together as one people, sharing the same sort of spirit-level connection with each other as we share with Jesus. Furthermore, we can see that as a people we are together in Christ, just as we are individually in Christ.

We don't need to circle anything because we've finally gotten to the point where we can talk about the whole picture, our unity with each other and with Jesus in the heavens. This is taught in the Scriptures in numerous places, some of which we've seen before, and they are worth revisiting in view of all we've studied so far.

> *For even as the body is one and yet has many members, and all the members of the body, though they are many, are one body, so also is Christ. For by one Spirit we were all baptized into one body, whether Jews or Greeks, whether slaves or free, and we were all made to drink of one Spirit.*
> **1 Corinthians 12:12-13**

In these verses, we see Paul again using the word baptism in the spiritual sense of having gone through the immersion of death with Jesus. This is something we all went through together, simultaneously. In keeping with that, we all partake of the same Holy Spirit. The Holy Spirit is not apportioned between us, but rather is complete within all of us. He provides the divine linkage between all believers, and between all of us and Jesus.

> *For just as we have many members in one body and all the members do not have the same function, so we, who are many, are one body in Christ, and individually members one of another.*
> **Romans 12:4-5**

Here, Paul refers to the Church as a body with many members, who are all one body in Christ. We recall from the previous chapter that being *in Christ* expresses the highest level of union possible. This is what Jesus asked of God for us in John 17, that we should be one with Him as He is one with the Father. Here, Paul is saying that we are one body of people with a union as close with each other as that which Jesus and the Father share. If it doesn't seem that way at times, it is because we are looking at earthly things rather than the Things Above. However, we are setting our minds on the Things Above, to see what they are, and the Scriptures so far appear to be teaching us a deep, rich truth concerning our unity.

> *For all of you who were baptized into Christ have clothed yourselves with Christ. There is neither Jew nor Greek, there is neither slave nor free man, there is neither male nor female; for you are all one in Christ Jesus.*
> **Galatians 3:27-28**

Despite any ethnic, status, or gender differences, all believers are one in Christ due to having undergone baptism into Christ. The union we have in Jesus transcends all visible differences because it is true in our spirits where the Holy Spirit resides.

Paul also alludes to the unity we have with each other in the following passage:

> *For even though I am absent in body, nevertheless I am with you in spirit, rejoicing to see your good discipline and the stability of your faith in Christ.*
> **Colossians 2:5**

This is not merely a nice sentiment. Paul is not saying he has them in his heart and thinks about them often. He is tapping directly into the truth that we are genuinely one with each other at the spirit level. He knows he is with them in spirit because that is consistent with the rest of his theology about unity. The fact that he says this to people he has never met makes it even more profound.

What does this mean for us on earth? It means that we are one with every believer in our church, every believer in our city, and every believer around the world. We have the same spirit level union with them as we have with Jesus. We all share the same spiritual relationship, created in Christ by God. We were immersed into Jesus in His death. When He was on the cross, He reached out through time and space to join all of us to Himself, *and* all of us to each other. The Holy Spirit cements this union – we all drink of the same Holy Spirit.

Common Challenges to Unity

Sadly, we are so accustomed to disunity that we barely believe there can be a better way. In our churches and our relationships with other believers, we are often pulling in different directions, with all kinds of attitudes and unspoken criticisms between us. Because it is natural and familiar, we think it is normal for us. Our experience tells us that our unity in Christ can't be true, but the Things Above say otherwise. Scripture teaches this about us, regardless of what we see.

Why does it seem so rare to experience anything near the kind of closeness we ought to expect, given this truth? There are at least four reasons for disunity that have been common to all churches since the time of the apostles.

First, we are all at different stages of growth in our walks with God. In any given church there is commonly a range of different maturity levels. Ideally there are mature believers. These should be helping the less mature to grow in Christ, but it does not always happen. There are often numerous people in the process of maturing. There may be yet more people that believe, want to be better at the Christian life, but simply haven't made much progress yet. There should also be new believers, who barely know what the Christian life is about and scarcely know the Scriptures. Add to this mix the many people that have never believed the Gospel, and you have a potent mix of differences.

In such a context, disunity can arise in several ways. Young believers often have little insight into authority and can pull in their own direction, or even resist or oppose those in authority. Pride may cause some believers to look down on others. Gossip, slander, and backbiting can take hold. Just about any sin can disrupt unity and cause divisions.

Second, cultural differences can be a source of disunity. Cultural differences can arise between differing age groups, ethnic groups, socioeconomic classes, or anything else. Cultural differences upset the Hellenistic Jews in Acts 6, and acted as a wedge issue in several of the churches to which Paul wrote. They still act as a major dividing force in churches today.

Third, theological differences can become a source of disunity. Theological differences have been at the root of countless church splits, although they do not always reach that level of intensity and polarization. More commonly such differences simply separate believers that take exception to each other's beliefs, and who then allow this to evolve into division. People separate themselves from others based on various points of theology or practice while disregarding the larger truths about which we all agree. In doing so they reject what God's Word says about our unity in Christ. Such divisions can be along familiar areas of dispute, such as spiritual gifts, eschatological views, baptism, etc., or about lesser points of doctrine or practice. Any point of doctrine can serve as a source of division if it is allowed to evolve from disagreement to sinful criticism and rejection of others.[16]

Fourth, personality differences can come into play even among the most mature believers. There will always be people whose outlook, ways, and mannerisms are beyond our comprehension. Some people seem almost designed to annoy us, trying our patience at every turn. There will always be such people in the church, and that is fine; we need such people to rub the edges off us. They are the ones that should remind us to draw near to God and abide in Christ rather than sin by rejecting them.

The Necessity of Unity

Despite these inevitable challenges, our spiritual unity remains true about us. It was at great cost that Jesus joined Himself to us and became the means by which we were joined to each other. When we look past the problems and instead learn what the Scriptures teach, we

---

[16] This is not to say that there are no doctrines on which we take a stand. On the contrary, we have espoused the centrality of the Scriptures as the final authoritative guide for faith and practice. It is the measure of our lives. Some people reject this at great peril to themselves, but they are never to be regarded as our enemies. To the Christian, nobody is an enemy, as Paul makes clear in Ephesians 6:12, "For our struggle is not against flesh and blood." People may endeavor to be enemies to us, but we are never to be enemies to them, rather we are to pray for them, for their good. The entrance into the Kingdom of God is wide enough for all who respond to God as King and Father in accordance with His Word, and hold to Christ alone as their hope of salvation.

find that God did an amazing work through Jesus to make us one in Him. We *are* actually joined spiritually to one another. Therefore, it should not surprise us that when issues of unity are addressed in the Scriptures, we are not so much told to *be unified* as we are commanded to *maintain* the unity we already have.

> *Therefore I, the prisoner of the Lord, implore you to walk in a manner worthy of the calling with which you have been called, with all humility and gentleness, with patience, showing tolerance for one another in love, being diligent to preserve the unity of the Spirit in the bond of peace. There is one body and one Spirit, just as also you were called in one hope of your calling; one Lord, one faith, one baptism, one God and Father of all who is over all and through all and in all.*
> **Ephesians 4:1-6**

The command of interest to us here is to *preserve* the unity of the Spirit. Unity has been established for us in Christ. Thus, we are not commanded to generate, or create unity. Rather we are to *preserve* it. Much of the rest of the the the passage refers to the Things Above, assuring us of the basis for the command.

But there is more. We are to *be diligent* to preserve the unity of the Spirit. Attaining unity on earth takes focused effort. It is not something that will just happen if we gather together. We do many things to promote unity in our churches. We have communal worship, we pray for each other, we have potluck meals, we serve in projects together, and so on. These are certainly good things, but they are no replacement for repentance, confession, prayer, and abiding in Christ. Only these things can overcome the common challenges to unity discussed above.

In terms of providing evidence to unbelievers that Jesus really is the Savior from God, unity is critical, and it is precisely in the area of unity that the rubber hits the road. It is here that diligence is most necessary. Congregations need to hear frequently how important it is. Leaders need to be models of diligence in this area, something they will only be if it is central to their vision of the Kingdom of God.

Not surprisingly, then, in speaking of unity in the Church, Paul says to the Corinthians…

Now I exhort you, brethren, by the name of our Lord Jesus Christ, that you all agree and that there be no divisions among you, but that you be made complete in the same mind and in the same judgment.
1 Corinthians 1:10

We are to be of the same mind. What mind is that?

For who has known the mind of the Lord, that he will instruct Him? But we have the mind of Christ.
1 Corinthians 2:16

It is the mind of Christ. But how can we have the mind of Christ unless we are abiding in Christ, and have been diligent at preserving the unity of the Spirit? So again, the command is not to *be unified*. Rather we are to behave in such as way as not to damage unity, because we *are unified*. The Corinthians had allowed false notions to divide them along fictitious lines. Paul's answer was to point them back to the centrality of Jesus. They were disagreeing about foolish things and it was tearing them apart. They had set their minds on earthly things, rather than on the Things Above. Turning their minds toward Christ, to have His mind about their unity, was Paul's solution.

Once again, Paul counsels the Philippian believers to live in light of the unity that they already have:

Therefore if there is any encouragement in Christ, if there is any consolation of love, if there is any fellowship of the Spirit, if any affection and compassion, make my joy complete by being of the same mind, maintaining the same love, united in spirit, intent on one purpose. Do nothing from selfishness or empty conceit, but with humility of mind regard one another as more important than yourselves; do not merely look out for your own personal interests, but also for the interests of others.
Philippians 2:1-4

In this passage there is no question about whether there is encouragement in Christ, or consolation through the love we have received, or fellowship of the Spirit. These are found in Christ, among the Things Above. Paul mentions them to focus attention on the very things that provide the basis for unity in the first place. The command is that we do the things that uphold unity among us on earth, and stop doing the things that destroy it like being selfish and conceited.

Paul's consistent approach to unity is to teach the underlying truth of our connectedness to each other and to Jesus. He exhorts believers to live purposefully as though that is true, laying aside hurtful speech and divisions of all kinds.

Unity and the Kingdom Way

How do we apply all this? The same way we apply all the Things Above. We combine Scripture-based action with faith-filled prayer. Our actions begin with believing what the Scriptures teach us about our unity. All of us, I would guess, can find much about which to repent when we take these truths about unity deep down into us. We have all been guilty of allowing the common challenges described above to wear away or destroy the unity that we are meant to experience and uphold. Repentance may mean reconciling with others, humbling ourselves to others, reaching out to those different from ourselves. We are tasked with doing all in our power to restore relationships within the Body of Christ. Just as Jesus says:

> *Therefore if you are presenting your offering at the altar, and there remember that your brother has something against you, leave your offering there before the altar and go; first be reconciled to your brother, and then come and present your offering.*
> **Matthew 5:23-24**

Jesus commanded people to reconcile with each other even if that meant leaving a sacrifice on the altar. Reconciliation is given a higher value in the Kingdom of God than offerings. It is urgent, so we must act with a sense of urgency. The alternative is to allow (for ourselves, or for the other party) the sun to go down on our anger yet again, something we are elsewhere commanded not to do.

How do you know if you need to reconcile with someone? One good way to tell is to look at the Things Above.

In detail, our relationships with one another in the heavenly Kingdom look like this. We are one with each other through the work of Jesus and the Holy Spirit. We are in Him, and we are joined to each other. So when you consider a brother or sister in Christ, if you can't envision them this way, if there are unresolved issues between you, or if you don't desire to be in harmony with them, there is likely a need for reconciliation. If there is unholiness or unrighteousness in the relationship, the Holy Spirit will be hindered in helping you have unity with that person. In the heavens you are unified, but it is impossible to experience that on earth as in heaven because of the unresolved issues between you.

But consider that Jesus is the minister of our reconciliation with God. He is also ready, through His Spirit, to be the minister of reconciliation between yourself and others when He finds readiness to live the Kingdom Way. Obedience through repentance and reconciliation is critical to restoring unity. Successful repentance requires dedication to the Word, obedience to God as King, acceptance of His grace as Father, confession of all past sins, abiding in Christ for power to do otherwise, and, all along, considerable amounts of prayer.

The sins that lead to disunity and division are no different than any others. We are merely examining them as a specific category that is destructive of one of the key components of the Kingdom of God, the expression of our unity on earth as in heaven. That we all, individually, have a role to play in restoring and maintaining unity should be clear by now. We must act biblically to be obedient to this vision, this truth.

But as with all the Things Above, the Kingdom Way teaches us we must also pray. In this case individual and corporate prayer are both important. There are also a variety of outcomes that we are to obtain through prayer. The chart below summarizes them. We will discuss each point as numbered.

	Our Relationships	Others' Relationships	Broader Unity
Individual Prayer (1)	Pray individually for restoration and harmony within our own set of relationships. (2)	Pray individually for restoration and harmony in the relationships of specific people we know. (3)	Pray individually and corporately for deeper unity that demonstrates the Holy Spirit's presence in our midst (6), and to overcome inter-church divisions so that the Church is unified at the city level. (7)
Corporate Prayer (4)	Pray corporately that all relationships in the church, including our own, would be restored and maintained in harmony through the Holy Spirit. (5)		

First, I am assuming at this point in our study of the Kingdom of God that we are convinced about the centrality of prayer where achieving God's purposes is concerned. This is no less true where unity and reconciliation are concerned. Remember that Jesus and the Holy Spirit intercede for us, and that our unity on earth is of considerable importance to them. We can be confident that when we pray for unity we are joining with them in their prayers for us that God's will be done through unity.

Second, we must personally have a focus on restoring and maintaining unity in our own relationships. This should be an obvious emphasis when we consider the many "one another" commands in the Bible, such as love on another and pray for one another. Prayer is important to our individual relationships because it is the means by which we obtain God's involvement in our endeavors to restore and maintain unity. Going to others to seek restoration may require humbling ourselves and confessing sins to them. Jesus can provide the wisdom and spiritual preparation we need in such circumstances.

Third, we are often aware of poor relationships and disunity between others. We have a personal obligation as members of the same body to be individually praying for their restoration and healing. We suffer when others are at odds, because, almost invariably, there is sin involved. Where there is sin, there will, of course, be residual unrighteousness and all that goes with it in terms of reduced effectiveness in service. Just as Paul says:

> *And if one member suffers, all the members suffer with it; if one member is honored, all the members rejoice with it.*
> **1 Corinthians 12:26**

The effect may be subtle, or it may be quite obvious and disruptive. Either way, it works against the harmony we should have in the body. It also reduces the freedom of the Holy Spirit to work though us as Christ's body. The role of individual prayer in the restoration of relationships is critical. Peacemakers are given a specific blessing in the Sermon on the Mount.

> *Blessed are the peacemakers, for they shall be called sons of God.*
> **Matthew 5:9**

The heart of a peacemaker is one that is in touch with Jesus' desire for unity among His people.

Fourth, one only needs to read Acts to notice that most of the greatest movements of God were preceded by corporate prayer. So far we have focused on prayer as it bears on the restoration and preservation of unity, but that is not the only purpose of communal prayer. Corporate prayer is beautifully modeled for us in Acts, and the passages are worth studying at length. One thing we learn is that there is something powerful about believers praying together in unity to ask great things of God. Corporate prayer has power that individual prayer lacks, and God seems to honor it with bigger results. This is perfectly understandable when we look at the heavenly Kingdom, where we are all one, united by the Holy Spirit, and in union with Jesus *as He makes His requests* to the father. Communal prayer was central to the practice of those in the Early Church and it should be for us as well.

Oliver W. Price has written an excellent book entitled, *The Power of Praying Together: Experiencing Christ Actively in Charge*[17] in which he emphasizes four key components that contribute to effective corporate prayer. Paraphrasing, they are:

- Asking Jesus to be present just as He promises He will be.
- Trusting Him to take charge as the head of His Church.
- Being willing for Him to change each of us as He sees fit.
- Being willing for Him to bring us all into harmony with the Father.

We can immediately see these principles are consistent with our understanding of the Kingdom of God, and can add to these the fact that we are *one people* in the Lord. Since we have, *together*, been joined to Jesus and the Holy Spirit, and both of Them intercede for us, our correct response on earth is to *join together in joining with Them* in prayer. Corporate prayer can be the highest expression of our unity, an activity in which we can beautifully express and participate in our unity with each other, Jesus, and the Holy Spirit. This concept is central to the effectiveness of corporate prayer, and why we so often read about it in Acts. Among the disciplines that the modern church needs to recover, few exceed this one in importance.

Fifth, it is everyone's responsibility to look after the health of the Body. Corporate prayer should be directed toward the unity of the body. Just like other aspects of the Kingdom, we need God's miraculous intervention for unity to come about. Unity is of God, and takes His supernatural involvement to thrive among us. Enlisting the body to pray for our reconciliation with others is a humble, sensible thing to do. When we have a relationship that is troubled, the need for

---

[17] While corporate prayer is an obvious application from our study of the Kingdom of God and a critical function of the Church, we will not delve into practical aspects of how to cultivate it in churches. Books like Price's help fill this gap. I highly recommend it as a practical guide to corporate prayer for all kinds of situations. It is a good starting point for those wishing to strengthen corporate prayer.

God to act can be great. Bringing this to others, tactfully, discretely, and anonymously, if needed, is an important part of restoring unity within the body. Public confession of sins in this context also increases the effectiveness of our prayers because God sees us doing things in accordance with His Kingdom.

Sixth, what we are really seeking is the free movement of the Holy Spirit in our midst. We want God to have freedom to speak directly to us as a body of believers, as He did in Antioch.

> *While they were ministering to the Lord and fasting, the Holy Spirit said, "Set apart for Me Barnabas and Saul for the work to which I have called them."*
> **Acts 13:2**

This sort of unity transcends the mere absence of divisions, just as abiding in Christ is more than mere freedom from unrighteousness. Unity of this sort is a powerful, positive outworking of the Holy Spirit among the people of God. In fact, this kind of harmony with the Spirit of Jesus Christ is the corporate equivalent of abiding in Christ. It is in this context that God principally desires to guide us, sanctify us, and minister to others through us. Believers can reach such a point of harmony with God that He is able to disclose His will to us, just as He did in Antioch. Paul describes this state of unity beautifully.

> *Now may the God who gives perseverance and encouragement grant you to be of the same mind with one another according to Christ Jesus, so that with one accord you may with one voice glorify the God and Father of our Lord Jesus Christ.*
> **Romans 15:5-6**

When this sort of unity exists among believers, we truly become the Body of Christ in the sense that He obtains a people through whom He Himself can minister. These days it is a rare thing, but we should think of it as a normal and desirable expression of God's Kingdom, one that we should pursue with great diligence and much prayer. In fact, Paul is praying here. He is asking God to bring this about among the Roman believers, which shows just how critical God's involvement is for this to come about.

Seventh, we are to pray for and pursue unity with all believers in our cities. We will delve into this in greater depth in chapter eight. Suffice it to say that there is a particular emphasis on cities in the Bible. The Church occupies a place of great importance in a city, one that is best expressed and most empowered when divisions between local bodies of believers are set aside, allowing the larger community of believers to function as one people at the city level.

As we can see, the Kingdom of God provides many reasons why prayer, especially communal prayer, is essential for God's people. So why does prayer fail in churches? Here are a just dozen reasons.

Reasons Prayer Fails	Relevant Scriptures
There is no compelling positive vision for it.	Colossians 3:1-2 – The Things Above
There is no compelling sense that it is sin not to pray communally.	Matthew 6:9 – Jesus commands us to pray.
People come expecting rapid results and quit when they don't see any.	Luke 18:1-8 – Persistence counts.
People are praying for their will to be done, not God's, so no blessings come.	Matthew 6:10 – "Your will be done."
Church leadership does not model or promote prayer, so people disregard it.	Galatians 6:7 – What leadership sows, it will reap.
The Holy Spirit led, but was not obeyed.	Colossians 1:9-10 – We are to know God's will, and do it.
There is no willingness among participants to be changed by God.	Hebrews 12:11 – We should expect the Lord to be working on us, and let Him.
New people who come are ignored by the group, and never return.	1 Corinthians 12:12 – We are one body.
Jesus and the Holy Spirit have not been invited or welcomed.	Exodus 33:15-16 – His presence among us is critical.
There are unresolved sin issues between people in the group.	1 Peter 3:7 – Sin can hinder our prayers.
People come because of guilt, not love.	Mark 12:30 – You shall love the Lord, so go be with Him.
There is unconfessed sin among the individuals or within the Body.	James 5:16 – We are to confess our sins.

This should be considered a partial list. Church leadership should be mindful of theses pitfalls as they model and promote communal prayer.

The Larger Goal

As we can see, Kingdom centered prayer for unity is a multifaceted matter. God wants the fullness of His will to be brought about on earth as in heaven, and we see in the heavens that His will regarding unity is expansive, beautiful, and powerful. However, we should not lose sight of the reason Jesus sought this unity. Recall Jesus' prayer:

> *I do not ask on behalf of these alone, but for those also who believe in Me through their word; that they may all be one; even as You, Father, are in Me and I in You, that they also may be in Us, so that the world may believe that You sent Me.*
> **John 17:20-21**

All aspects of our union with Christ are provided so that the world will believe Jesus came from the Father. What does the world need to see in order to understand that? One of the main things is love. A common criticism is that we believers are always fighting amongst ourselves. All too often this is a valid assessment. Unity within the body of Christ is meant to overcome division and provide supernatural evidence that cannot be denied, so that men are without excuse. When unbelievers look at believers and see powerful love from the Holy Spirit in our midst, they recognize they are in the presence of Christ and their excuses fall flat. Our communal life in Christ is to convince others about Jesus.

> *By this all men will know that you are My disciples, if you have love for one another.*
> **John 13:35**

> *Beyond all these things put on love, which is the perfect bond of unity. Let the peace of Christ rule in your hearts, to which indeed you were called in one body; and be thankful.*
> **Colossians 3:14-15**

Thus, unity is not a goal in its own right. We are not meant to simply be together and be unified, apart from the eyes of the world, like monks in a monastery. We are on display to the world as Christ's body. What they see among us, they will believe about Jesus. The absence of the love of God among us is a betrayal of our own stated goal of reaching the lost. However, when a Scripture-based vision of the Kingdom of God and His will for us drives us toward individual and corporate confession and repentance, when reconciliation and harmony are high values among the people of God, and when corporate prayer is earnestly and regularly devoted to calling on God to build unity among us, the Holy Spirit has free reign to move powerfully among us and preach Jesus to peoples' hearts, so that they come to repentance and belief. As Paul says:

> *Finally, brethren, rejoice, be made complete, be comforted, be like-minded, live in peace; and the God of love and peace will be with you.*
> **2 Corinthians 13:11**

In keeping with this, we see Paul praying more than once for love to grow among believers.

> *And this I pray, that your love may abound still more and more in real knowledge and all discernment, so that you may approve the things that are excellent, in order to be sincere and blameless until the day of Christ; having been filled with the fruit of righteousness which comes through Jesus Christ, to the glory and praise of God.*
> **Philippians 1:9-11**

> *And may the Lord cause you to increase and abound in love for one another, and for all people, just as we also do for you*
> **1 Thessalonians 3:12**

Paul knows that unless there is prayer specifically devoted to love and unity, they won't happen. We can now see why it is critically important that they *do* happen. Without these, we will never be as effective at reaching people for Christ. In addition, we will miss out on untold joys we are meant to have through communal fellowship with each other and Christ. A Holy Spirit-unified people *will* convince others about Jesus.

Conclusion

We are unified with all other believers and with Jesus in the heavens. For God's will to be done here, we must put aside the things that destroy unity and call upon God for Him to bring about the heavenly unity that characterizes the relationships that He has established for us in Christ. He wants a people that abide in Him, are sanctified in Him, and minister together in His power. Through such a people, Jesus can overcome unbelief, convincing the lost of His identity as the Son of God and the Savior for all people. Unity among believers is central to His methods.

Challenges

If you have a hard time viewing a brother or sister in Christ as one with you in Christ, you may have some reconciliation to do. Begin applying all the kingdom principles we have learned so far, starting with accepting the truth of God's Word about your true relationship with that person, confessing any sins, abiding in Christ while endeavoring to do His will, and praying for God's involvement in all aspects of your reconciliation. Then go do it.

Pray regularly for the unity of the church. If you are a leader of any sort, lead prayer for unity frequently.

If you have events planned to build unity, recognize that a successful event in itself will not necessarily improve unity if God is not also supernaturally involved in bringing unity forth from heaven in answer to your prayers. True fellowship is a product of unity, not the reverse. Prayer is essential.

If you are a song leader, you have a role to play in reinforcing the truth of our unity. Substitute "we" for "I" as appropriate in songs sung by the congregation.

If communal prayer has not been a part of your life, join an existing prayer group. Start one, if needed, in order to meet this need. Find like-minded people that will dedicate themselves to communal prayer and persevere in praying for others to join you, and for unity to come from the Lord. Be open to believers from other churches, or join an existing prayer group in another church. They are your brethren in Christ.

Read Oliver Price's book, *The Power of Praying Together: Experiencing Christ Actively in Charge*. This book provides excellent guidance on corporate prayer in many different situations.

Discuss and answer these questions: If Jesus is praying and the Holy Spirit is praying, what should we be doing if God's will is to be done on earth as in heaven? Is personal devotional time alone a sufficient response to the Things Above where prayer is concerned?

Takedown

Joel and Amy walked out of the restaurant, to-go bags in hand. They heard sirens approaching a short way off and looked up the street to their left. Flashing lights were moving toward them. Blocks away, and in the lead, a dark SUV sped toward the intersection before them.

"Check it out," Joel said.

They watched, spellbound, as the SUV swerved this way and that, dodging cars. Amy looked at the traffic light over the intersection in front of her. It was green and traffic was flowing through it. A car was turning onto the main street from the side road next to her.

A block away now, the SUV had an open road. Amy could hear the engine rev as the driver gunned it toward the intersection. Looking back at the intersection, Amy's heart jumped in her throat as a car turned left across the path of the SUV toward the side street. Too late, the driver saw the approaching SUV and hit the brakes, stopping almost dead in the intersection.

The SUV corrected wildly, swerved onto the curb in front of them. The right front end hit the concrete pedestal of a streetlight. It spun clockwise into the intersection. The passenger side slammed into the front of the stopped car, shoving it backward. The SUV stopped, facing back up the street toward the police. Its front end was demolished, the right wheel askew.

Joel and Amy could see the driver moving within the SUV. He was rubbing his face with his hands.

Seconds later three police cars pulled up at the edge of the intersection. Turning left across the lanes to make cover for themselves, each parked with its passenger side facing the SUV. Officers emerged and positioned themselves behind their cars. More sirens could be heard in the distance.

"Hey, get in here. If things get ugly, you don't want to be out there." They both startled at the voice. Looking behind them, a man was holding the door for them to come back into the restaurant. "Not a safe place if the lead starts flying."

"Uh, yeah, thanks," Joel said, and the two went back inside.

The man was addressing the diners. "Everybody get back from the windows. Go on, move back. Glass won't stop a bullet." Several got up and moved back. Others stayed put.

Joel and Amy moved further in but found a place to watch the scene outside.

A fourth police car had pulled up behind the first three. One of the police was using a PA to talk to the driver of the SUV. Amy couldn't hear the words because of the music in the restaurant. She could still see the driver of the SUV moving. He was leaning over toward the passenger side and moving slightly.

Several of the officers had their guns drawn and were crouched behind the front or rear wheels of their cars. Something moved to her right and Amy saw an officer had run around the side of the drive-thru and was now crouched behind the brick base of the restaurant's sign, gun drawn.

"Let's move further back," she said to Joel, and they did, finding a better place behind the salad bar. She couldn't see the police cars very well now, but could see the driver had cracked open his door. He appeared to be yelling back at the police, who were still addressing him with the PA. She still couldn't hear what was being said.

"Ya'll get back from the windows. He's got a gun! Get back and get some cover." It was the same man. He stood behind a pillar in the dining area and quickly peaked out toward the street from time to time. More people moved, some crouching. Nobody was at the windows now.

Amy looked back out. She thought she could see the driver's mouth moving. Yelling, she supposed, but the glare and distance made it hard to tell.

The standoff went on for several minutes with little change. The driver's door was still cracked open. The PA could be heard now – someone had turned off the music in the restaurant.

"Drop the gun and put your hands up through the door."

The driver said something nobody could hear.

"No. You are surrounded. Drop the gun and put your hands up through the door. Remain in your car and drop your gun."

The driver yelled back again.

"You have no options here. If you aim the gun, you will be fired upon. Drop the gun and put your hands up through the door."

A cloud shadow moved over the area and Amy could see the driver now. The back of his left hand was against the window of the driver's door. He held a pistol that was aimed upward. He might have been talking on a cell phone. His mouth moved but she couldn't hear anything.

"Put down the phone, drop your gun on the street and put both hands up through the door. If you aim the gun you will be fired upon."

The driver threw his phone to the floor and pounded the dashboard with his right fist. His hand with the gun could not be seen. Amy looked to the right and saw the officer behind the sign looking tense and focused on the driver.

Looking back, she could see the driver was now putting his face on his right hand on the steering wheel.

"You are surrounded. Drop the gun to the street and put both hands up through the door. If you aim the gun, we will fire on you. Drop the gun."

Sitting up, the driver looked out his side window, seemed to see the officer behind the sign, and hung his head, shaking it from side to side.

Tension built as decision hung in the air. A silent moment went by.

Looking up, he nodded. His gun fell to the street. He put both hands up through the open door and waited.

Amy saw two officers moving carefully toward the SUV, approaching it from the front, guns drawn on the driver. The driver's hands stayed up through the door.

"Remain still with your hands up. Do not move," came the voice over the PA again.

The driver remained motionless with his hands up, facing forward. One officer slowly approached the door, while another stood slightly crouched directly in front of the SUV with his gun trained on the driver. The first officer reached the gun and kicked it under the SUV, then backed up, holstering his gun.

Now, the first officer was speaking to the driver. The door opened further. The driver stepped out with his hands up. He had a bloody nose. He stepped forward again and began to crouch as though to get on the ground. The first officer moved in quickly, as well as a second from behind the SUV. They got the driver on the ground and were kneeling on his back as they handcuffed him.

"Whew! That was wild. Never seen anything like that before," Joel said, laughing nervously.

"Yeah. Wow! That was crazy," Amy answered. The whole restaurant seemed to relax. People were talking, laughing, moving around again. Some took seats by the windows to watch the show wind down outside. "Glad that guy got us to come in. I'd probably still be standing out there with my mouth hanging open!"

"No kidding!" said Joel. "You think you know what you'd do in a situation like that, but when it happens…" he trailed off.

"Exactly," Amy said. "It's a different story entirely."

Chapter 7

Kingdom Authority

And Jesus came up and spoke to them, saying,
"All authority has been given to Me in heaven
and on earth. Matthew 28:18

We are in the midst of a study on how the Church as a whole relates to the heavenly Kingdom of God. We've seen that unity means more than just getting along and doing things together. It is to be a powerful, positive, visible expression of Christ's love that is convincing to those looking on. Church unity is the context through which Jesus, as the head of the Church, communicates with His people and works in the world.

But there is an additional facet of Church unity that we cannot understand without understanding how authority is structured in the heavens, and how Jesus delegates authority to His Church to accomplish His purposes in the world. We need to take a major side road to understand authority in the heavens, which will be the subject of this chapter. In the following chapter, we will return to our discussion of unity and see how authority and unity interrelate at the city level.

But what do I mean by authority? The concept is best understood by answering the question "Who tells whom what to do?" This is the basis for interpreting earthly authority structures when one does not have an organizational chart in hand. With this question in mind we could go to most offices, walk the streets of most towns and cities, and look at most families and determine where authority lies based on peoples' interactions with each other. We would also see that there are different kinds of authority that overlap in specific and limited ways. Civil authority does not extend within the doors of households to influence how chores are assigned, but does extend into households when what is done in the household is also a crime, such as child abuse or murder. Church authority includes the right to discipline church members, but does not extend to those outside the church. Neither does church authority extend within the doors of the households of believers. The church cannot overrule the authority of parents to order their households as they choose if the issue is not one of sin. Similarly my employer's authority does not extend to my use of my personal time, where I take vacations, and what hobbies I enjoy. Each authority has its proper sphere, its jurisdiction.

In this chapter we will be studying the sphere of spiritual authority in the heavens. For a time we will leave behind our image of the Things Above and turn our attention to this separate but intimately related theme. Our goal is to understand the complex environment of spiritual authority in which we live. We will examine the Scriptures to see who is telling whom what to do, and from that we will build an organizational chart for the heavens. To start we'll need a list of the various entities we are concerned about in the realm of spiritual authority. They are:

- The Father
- Jesus
- The Holy Spirit
- Saved People
- Angels
- Satan
- Demons
- Unsaved People

As we study the authority relationships between all these entities, we will be tempted to explore all the implications of the various verses immediately, but we'll forego some of that for now. Our goal is a comprehensive view of authority, so we'll be looking at things in the broadest terms. We will focus more narrowly once we have an organizational chart in which we are confident.

Authority in the Godhead

We'll start at the top, since the authority relationships within the Godhead are among the clearest.

> *Jesus said to them again, "Peace be with you. As the Father has sent me, even so I am sending you."*
> **John 20:21**

In this verse we see clearly that the Father sent Jesus. The Father has authority over the Son. He did the sending and Jesus did the obeying by going. The Father tells the Son what to do, and the Son does it. In our organizational chart, we can portray authority between them like this:

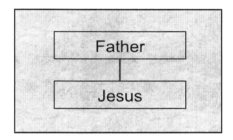

We see the same authority in verses like this:

> *I will no longer talk much with you, for the ruler of this world is coming. He has no claim on me, but I do as the Father has commanded me, so that the world may know that I love the Father. Rise, let us go from here.*
> **John 14:30-31**

Now, let's consider the Holy Spirit. Jesus clearly has authority over the Holy Spirit.

> *But I tell you the truth, it is to your advantage that I go away; for if I do not go away, the Helper will not come to you; but if I go, I will send Him to you.*
> **John 16:7**

God has raised this Jesus to life, and we are all witnesses of the fact. Exalted to the right hand of God, he has received from the Father the promised Holy Spirit and has poured out what you now see and hear.
Acts 2:32-33

Jesus asked the Father for the Holy Spirit and was given authority over Him by the Father. We have also seen previously that the Holy Spirit is sometimes called things like the Spirit of Jesus Christ.

At this point our chart looks like this:

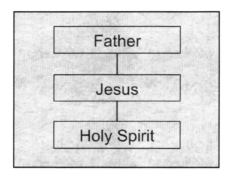

It is helpful to remember that we are not talking about the nature of the Trinity. God is triune, existing as three Persons having one essence. That is evident in many Scriptures. What we are looking at is how authority and responsibility have been divided among the three Persons of the Trinity. We clearly see them taking different roles and carrying out different tasks. When we look at the Trinity and ask "Who is telling Whom what to do," we see certain relationships of authority, and that is what we are portraying here.

Authority Among the Other Entities

The remaining entities are all covered by the following passage. We'll look at them with greater precision shortly, but just to be clear about the encompassing authority of Jesus…

These are in accordance with the working of the strength of [the Father's] might which He brought about in Christ, when He raised Him from the dead and seated Him at His right hand in the heavenly places, far above all rule and

authority and power and dominion, and every name that is named, not only in this age but also in the one to come. And He put all things in subjection under His feet, and gave Him as head over all things to the church, which is His body, the fullness of Him who fills all in all.
Ephesians 1:19b-23

This passage shows that Jesus has genuine authority over everything and everyone. Therefore the rest of the entities will have to work into the organizational chart below Jesus. We see this idea reflected in the following passage as well:

For this reason also, God highly exalted Him, and bestowed on Him the name which is above every name, so that at the name of Jesus every knee will bow, of those who are in heaven and on earth and under the earth, and that every tongue will confess that Jesus Christ is Lord, to the glory of God the Father.
Philippians 2:9-11

Starting with angels, we'll look at how authority is structured under Jesus' reign. Scripture seems to indicate there are at least two kinds of angels: angels and archangels. However, archangels are only mentioned once in the Scriptures, in Jude, and their relationship to the rest of the angels is unclear. It seems likely they have higher authority than angels, but it is not certain. Just to be careful, we will lump them together with angels.

Jesus Christ, who has gone into heaven and is at God's right hand—with angels, authorities and powers in submission to him.
1 Peter 3:21b-22

So, angels are subject to Jesus. This makes sense when we look at how angels interacted with Jesus.

Now an angel from heaven appeared to Him, strengthening Him.
Luke 22:43

Then the devil left him, and angels came and attended him.
Matthew 4:11

Angels served Jesus. Jesus also indicated He had authority to command angels if He so chose.

Do you think I cannot call on my Father, and he will at once put at my disposal more than twelve legions of angels?
Matthew 26:53

Now our organizational chart looks something like this:

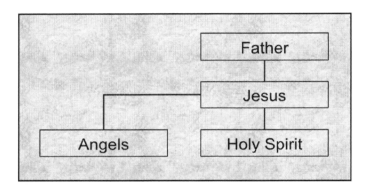

Next, we'll look at the other spirit beings, Satan and his demons. Satan was completely defeated by Jesus at the cross, as we see here:

And having disarmed the powers and authorities, he made a public spectacle of them, triumphing over them by the cross.
Colossians 2:15

And again in this verse:

Since the children have flesh and blood, he [Jesus] too shared in their humanity so that by his death he might destroy him who holds the power of death—that is, the devil.
Hebrews 2:14

This fits with what we saw above, where Jesus is stated to have authority over every name. We also understand from Scripture that Satan has a kingdom of his own, the kingdom of darkness, which includes demons.[18]

> *Then He will also say to those on His left, 'Depart from Me, accursed ones, into the eternal fire which has been prepared for the devil and his angels.'*
> **Matthew 25:41**

Jesus appears to validate this understanding by stating:

> *If Satan also is divided against himself, how will his kingdom stand? For you say that I cast out demons by Beelzebul.*
> **Luke 18:18**

In these passages we can see that Satan's kingdom includes the demons, and that they, too, now fall under Jesus' authority. Here is our chart with these latest additions:

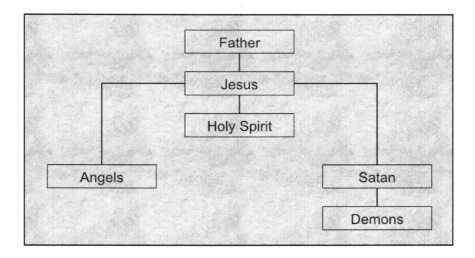

---

[18] The Bible never unequivocally states that demons are fallen angels. Both Matthew 25:41 and Revelation 12:9 mention "the devil and his angels," or something similar. This is as near as the Bible comes to indicating that demons are fallen angels. However, many scholars believe that demons originated as angels that joined with Satan in the rebellion against God, and to me that seems plausible.

If it seems strange to think of Satan as being under Jesus' authority, as though Jesus is in charge of evil, set that concern aside for the moment. When we finish the organizational chart, we'll examine that and other issues in greater detail.

Who else is in Satan's Kingdom? Sadly, unsaved people are under his authority, as these verses make clear.

> *The whole world is under the control of the evil one…*
> **1 John 5:19b**

> *And even if our Gospel is veiled, it is veiled to those who are perishing. The god of this age has blinded the minds of unbelievers, so that they cannot see the light of the Gospel of the glory of Christ, who is the image of God.*
> **2 Corinthians 4:3-4**

The god of this age is the devil. These verses make clear that he has authority to darken the minds of unbelievers and blind them to the truth. There is also a dominion of darkness, the kingdom Satan is endeavoring to set up for himself. Unsaved people remain in that kingdom, whereas we have been removed from it and transferred to another kingdom.

> *For [God] has rescued us from the dominion of darkness and brought us into the kingdom of the Son he loves, in whom we have redemption, the forgiveness of sins.*
> **Colossians 1:13**

The king over unsaved people is Satan, whereas ours is the Lord.

> *For such men are false apostles, deceitful workmen, masquerading as apostles of Christ. And no wonder, for Satan himself masquerades as an angel of light. It is not surprising, then, if his servants masquerade as servants of righteousness. Their end will be what their actions deserve.*
> **2 Corinthians 11:13-15**

Unbelievers are also servants of Satan. Some masquerade as Christians and attempt to deceive believers.

These verses and numerous others illustrate the terrible situation of unsaved people. They are citizens of Satan's kingdom rather than the Kingdom of God, and as such, they are under Satan's authority. Adding them to the chart, we have:

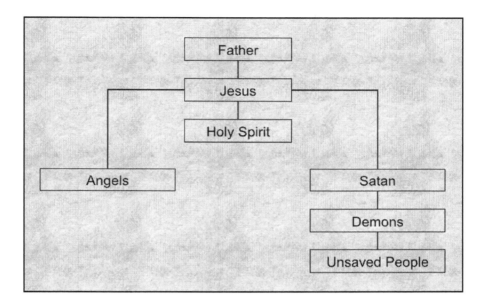

This is not to say that the unsaved are automatons under the complete and direct control of demons. What it does mean is that they are spiritually dead. They are slaves to sin, and are unable to enter relationship with God. To varying extents, mainly depending on the lies they believe and the residual unrighteousness they bear, they oppose and reject the things of God.

For saved people the situation is completely different. We are no longer under Satan. He is not our King. We are in a different kingdom, just as it says in Colossians 1:13, above. Paul's description of the mission given to him by God makes this even clearer.

> *"'I am sending you to them to open their eyes and turn them from darkness to light, and from the power of Satan to God, so that they may receive forgiveness of sins and a place among those who are sanctified by faith in me.'"*
> **Act 26:17b-18 NIV**

Paul was assigned to rescue people out of one kingdom and bring them into a better kingdom, God's. The result of that transfer, as we have seen, is our union with Jesus in the heavens.

> *And God raised us up with Christ and seated us with him in*
> *the heavenly realms in Christ Jesus.*
> **Ephesians 2:6**

And with that information we are nearly done with our organizational chart of spiritual authority.

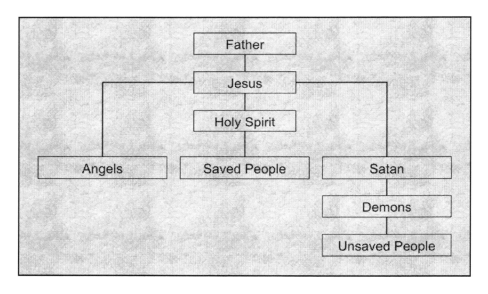

I say nearly done because although we have looked at all the different entities in our original list, this is still not the best representation we can make of spiritual authority. If we reflect back on previous chapters we recall that our connection with Jesus and the Holy Spirit has more to do with union than a mere linear relationship. We are *in Christ* and *in union with His Holy Spirit*. The best way to show this is by substituting our image of the Things Above into the chart like this:

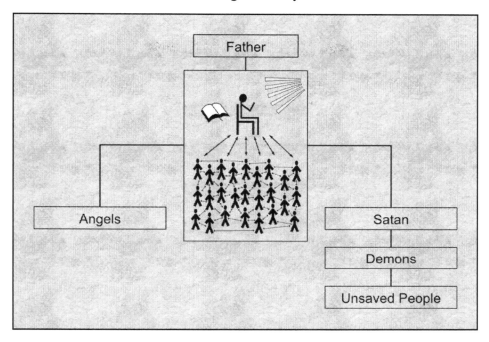

Clarifications

This is a better depiction of authority. We'll have much to say about it as we go on. However, I'd first like to address a few immediate concerns that may have arisen as we've pushed through to complete this chart. First and foremost, the organizational chart makes it look as though Jesus is directly supervising Satan. The relationship there is actually more complicated, so to make an analogy that will perhaps clarify things, let's think back to our understanding of our own relationship with Jesus.

We have already seen that we have all the righteousness of Jesus in the heavens through our redemption and union with Him. But we also know that is not the whole story for us. We are painfully aware that we do not walk in perfect righteousness here on earth despite our relationship with Jesus in the heavens. We've spent a great deal of time examining this issue and learning how Jesus provides what is needed to bring real change to this situation. He has given us confession of sins and abiding in Christ as powerful means by which to overcome sin and be transformed, so that we increasingly live like the people we are in the heavens.

In a manner of speaking, our flesh on earth is contested ground. Without any effort applied, without confession or abiding, we will go on in our sinful ways and miss many of the benefits of the great salvation we have been given. Our sinful tendencies will be uncontested. However, through confession and abiding, the outcome can be different. We can make war through Christ on our sinful selves and overcome them through Him. God's will is done on earth as in heaven when we act on these things.

The situation with Satan and his kingdom is similar. Jesus completely defeated Satan through His obedience to God. By living perfectly in the face of all temptations, He regained as a man the authority that mankind had lost by disobeying in the Garden so long ago. When He was raised into the heavens, God granted Him to sit in the seat of authority at His right hand. This signaled Satan's complete defeat, as is made clear by this verse:

> *When He had disarmed the rulers and authorities, He made a public display of them, having triumphed over them through Him.*
> **Colossians 2:15**

As I understand this, God disarmed the rulers and authorities, that is, Satan and his minions, through Jesus Christ. He then followed up this victory with something like a victory parade in the heavens in which Satan and his lot were publicly shamed. God's victory over Satan is complete. However, just as we are complete in Christ in the heavens, but have progress to make on earth, so also Satan is defeated in the heavens, but still fights on here on earth. Earth is contested ground, with Satan still opposing the rule of Christ here.

We can think of the situation like a sheriff. He has real authority within his jurisdiction, but that doesn't necessarily prevent people from breaking laws. Jesus is the rightful sheriff of the earth, but Satan and demons and people continue to break His laws. So the authority that Jesus won over Satan is real, but we do not yet see that entirely worked out on earth as in heaven yet. And that is exactly what the writer of Hebrews has to say:

*For in subjecting all things to him, He left nothing that is
not subject to him. But now we do not yet see all things
subjected to him.*
Hebrews 2:8b

All things were subjected to Jesus, but we do not see that yet. The
earthly domain remains contested ground, much as we ourselves are
contested ground. However, just as Jesus gave us all we need for life
and godliness through our union with Him, He has also given us all we
need to defeat Satan within our own spheres of authority, something
we will discuss in greater detail a bit later. Jesus by no means
supervises evil. He opposes it entirely. But Jesus' will is still in the
process of being worked out on earth.

Another area needing clarification is our relationship with angels. Our
last organizational chart seems to suggest that believers must possess
delegated authority over angels just as we possess delegated authority
over Satan and the demons. However, although we can often perceive
Satan's[19] influence in a situation, we rarely have any knowledge of
what angels are doing. We see this in several verses:

*For we wanted to come to you—I, Paul, more than once—
and yet Satan hindered us.*
1 Thessalonians 2:18

*Put on the full armor of God, so that you will be able to
stand firm against the schemes of the devil.*
Ephesians 6:11

Paul could distinguish the work of Satan from other sources of
difficulty, and taught that Satan has schemes that we should be able to
recognize, so as to stand firm against them.

*It happened that as we were going to the place of prayer, a
slave-girl having a spirit of divination met us, who was*

---

[19] We recognize that Satan, though powerful, is still only one spirit and is not
omnipresent. When we refer to "Satan" doing this or that, we are referring
generically to his kingdom, in full recognition that in the vast majority of
cases it is merely one of his demons. This is ordinary linguistic usage, similar
to saying "Hitler invaded Poland," when in fact Hitler himself stayed behind.

bringing her masters much profit by fortune-telling. Following after Paul and us, she kept crying out, saying, "These men are bond-servants of the Most High God, who are proclaiming to you the way of salvation." She continued doing this for many days. But Paul was greatly annoyed, and turned and said to the spirit, "I command you in the name of Jesus Christ to come out of her!" And it came out at that very moment.
Acts 16:16-18

Satan sometimes tips his hand through his involvement in acts of evil. This demonic spirit was identified and dealt with by Paul. Similar situations must have become clear every time the disciples cast out demons. The work of Satan's kingdom and servants is supposed to be recognizable by those who walk with God.

In contrast, the activities of angels are generally obscure to us. In the Old Testament certain activities are credited to them even when they have not visibly manifested themselves. During New Testament times, virtually the only accounts we have of them are when they have made themselves visible. We see no accounts of believers acting in authority over angels.

On the contrary, we are taught that angels are servants of believers, and we see them in this role ministering to Jesus.

Are not all angels ministering spirits sent to serve those who will inherit salvation.
Hebrews 1:14

And He was in the wilderness forty days being tempted by Satan; and He was with the wild beasts, and the angels were ministering to Him.
Mark 1:13

We also see angels fighting on behalf of God's people. In this case they are fighting to deliver a message to Daniel. The "kings of Persia" are widely thought to be spirit powers of darkness. They are distinguished from the leaders of Persia, who, elsewhere in Daniel, are clearly earthly rulers.

But the prince of the kingdom of Persia was withstanding me for twenty-one days; then behold, Michael, one of the chief princes, came to help me, for I had been left there with the kings of Persia.
Daniel 10:13

Fighting for us and ministering to us may be the two principle ways that angels operate, but they seem to do both on orders from above, not from men directly. Also, they generally seem to work behind the scenes, out of our view. There is no precedent in Scripture for humans commanding angels. On the contrary, Hebrews ranks Jesus much higher than angels. For this reason it is shameful to give angels glory and attention that should be given to the One that saved us. If angels are indeed commanded by Jesus to work secretly most of the time, then it must be His will for us not to know of their involvement. So instead of searching for evidence of them, we should keep…

fixing our eyes on Jesus, the author and perfecter of faith.
Hebrews 12:2a

For these reasons, I believe we do not have authority over angels, and I caution strongly against undue interest in them.

Delegation of Authority

Returning to our organizational chart, we should note that by integrating the Things Above into it, we are not diminishing the linear authority structure between Jesus, the Holy Spirit and ourselves. That authority is real regardless of the nearness we have to Jesus and His Spirit. However, constructing the chart that way illustrates that the authority Jesus has in the heavens can be understood as *delegated to us* through our union with Him. As mentioned above, Ephesians 1:19-22 makes clear that Jesus has authority over all other spiritual entities, including His Church. We are in union with Him *in that authority* through having been raised up and seated *in* Him:

But God, being rich in mercy, because of His great love with which He loved us, even when we were dead in our transgressions, made us alive together with Christ (by grace you have been saved), and raised us up with Him,

*and seated us with Him in the heavenly places in Christ
Jesus.*
Ephesians 2:4-6

Nothing at all prevents Him from delegating this authority to us, and
that is exactly what He has done for believers individually and for His
church. This is significant when we consider how God wants His will
to be done on earth as in heaven. Jesus is in heaven in full authority.
On earth, Satan has been permitted to fight on. Jesus has given us
heavenly authority on earth so that we can oppose Satan here. We are
to be instruments of His authority on earth as in heaven. We catch
glimpses of this in several passages in which New Testament believers
actually used this delegated authority.

> *The seventy returned with joy, saying, "Lord, even the
> demons are subject to us in Your name." And He said to
> them, "I was watching Satan fall from heaven like
> lightning. "Behold, I have given you authority to tread on
> serpents and scorpions, and over all the power of the
> enemy, and nothing will injure you. Nevertheless do not
> rejoice in this, that the spirits are subject to you, but rejoice
> that your names are recorded in heaven."*
> **Luke 10:17-19**

Jesus had sent the disciples out to minister in His name. When they
returned they reported excitedly that even demons were subject to
them *in Jesus' name*. We have already studied this phrase and
understood it to mean *as Jesus would*. In this case, they were using
authority *as Jesus would*, and since He had actually delegated that
authority to them, the results were the same. Thus, we can see that the
phrase *in Jesus' name* also encompasses His blessing and authority.
When the disciples cast out demons *in Jesus' name,* they did so *as He
would* do it, and did it *with His authority*.

The disciples continued to use authority in this way after the
resurrection as well, which proves that His delegation of such
authority was not limited to the time He was on earth. It remains in
place in the Present Day Kingdom of God.

> *The crowds with one accord were giving attention to what
> was said by Philip, as they heard and saw the signs which*

he was performing. For in the case of many who had unclean spirits, they were coming out of them shouting with a loud voice; and many who had been paralyzed and lame were healed.
Acts 8:6-7

And as we saw previously, Paul used delegated authority to drive the spirit of divination from the slave girl.

The use of delegated authority by believers fits perfectly with the outworking of God's heavenly Kingdom on earth. Satan, while defeated in the heavens, still has some latitude to work on earth. God's will is done on earth as in heaven when believers use the authority of Jesus to defeat Satan here. The principles of the Kingdom apply as expected.

Satan's Schemes

But there is more we can learn from our organizational chart. To make it easier to use we'll revert back to our original version of it.

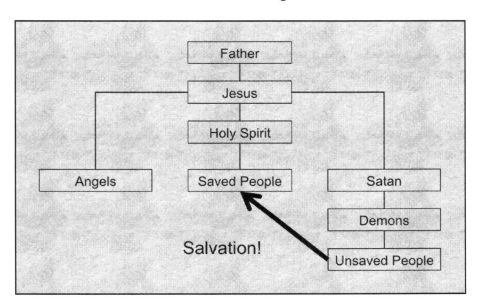

We should immediately notice that the spiritual environment in which we find ourselves is complex, with potential for numerous kinds of interactions between the various entities, some of whom have very different goals. We'll now explore what that means for us.

One thing that is clear is that when unsaved people get saved they are transferred from the rule of Satan's kingdom to the Kingdom of God. We see this in Colossians 1:13, as discussed above. This ought to impress us. The grace of God through Jesus Christ is powerful enough to effect a complete change of citizenship for those taken hold of by God. The victory of Christ is complete and irreversible!

However, regardless of how amazing that is, few new believers realize what has happened to them. Most have no idea how bad their situation was initially; nor how good it is afterward. Satan invariably tries to take advantage of this situation by continuing to whisper lies to them to the effect that they are still slaves of sin, that the promises of God can't be trusted, that they are, in fact, no different than they were before. He endeavors to tempt them into sins and undermine their confidence in God's promises, so as to gain or retain footholds in their lives. In other words, Satan, having lost kingdom rule over them, seeks to get them to live as though under his lordship anyway. This is his scheme against every believer, not just new ones. Zooming in on that part of the chart, Satan's activity can be seen this way.

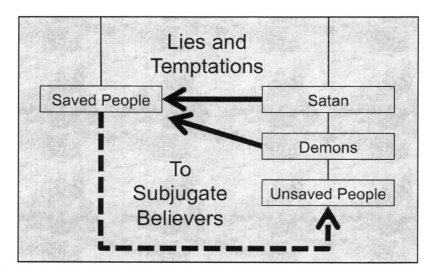

Here, Satan uses lies and temptations against saved people to subjugate them to his will, even though he has no real ownership of them anymore. He wants them to disbelieve promises God has made to them so they make no progress in their growth; he twists Scriptures to get them off on tangents, or even to get them believing that certain sins are perfectly allowable; and he tempts them directly through the world and by his own whispering. It is bad when he succeeds, and is completely unnecessary since we actually have been given all we need for life and godliness.

Do we see this in Scripture? Paul teaches that the Devil can gain footholds in our lives through our sins.

> *"In your anger do not sin": Do not let the sun go down while you are still angry, and do not give the devil a foothold.*
> **Ephesians 4:26-27 (NIV)**

It is certain that anger is not the only sin that can result in the devil gaining a foothold in one's life. The larger context of this passage includes admonitions to live obediently in other areas of life. We see this principle in the following passage as well, which describes one of the qualities needed in elders.

> *And he must have a good reputation with those outside the church, so that he will not fall into reproach and the snare of the devil.*
> **1 Timothy 3:7**

Elsewhere, Paul uses the phrase "snare of the devil" to describe the condition of unbelievers. The danger of falling back under the influence of Satan is quite real.

When we correctly understand a sin as choosing Satan's way rather than God's, we can easily see that any act of sin is a granting of obedience to Satan, a subtle but real granting of some lordship, something he welcomes. And, of course, the moment we sin we also gain a bit of residual unrighteousness. Remember that residual unrighteousness is a spiritual *substance* that clings to us. It is this substance that Satan holds onto in order to have a foothold, or grip, in our lives. The more unrighteousness we have, the stronger will be his grip. However, cleansing depletes Satan's license to work in our lives by diminishing his grip on us.

This adds a great deal of urgency to confession and helps explain why thorough confession of sins is such an effective way to reduce our tendency to sin. In fact, many breakthroughs in spiritual warfare occur through confession of sins. Consider the Ephesians:

> *Many of those who believed now came and openly confessed what they had done. A number who had practiced sorcery brought their scrolls together and burned them publicly. When they calculated the value of the scrolls, the total came to fifty thousand drachmas. In this way the word of the Lord spread widely and grew in power.*
> **Ephesians 19:18-20**

Their confession, repentance, and obedience resulted in a huge outflow of redemption.

The other way in which Satan seeks to influence us is by keeping us from surrendering areas of our lives to God. We know that God wants His Word to go into us and become a settled matter. When we encounter the Word of God in a new area of our lives and surrender to God, Satan loses a bit of influence in our lives. This is what Paul is getting at in Romans six.

> *Do you not know that when you present yourselves to someone as slaves for obedience, you are slaves of the one whom you obey, either of sin resulting in death, or of obedience resulting in righteousness?*
> **Romans 6:16**

God wants His lordship to increase in our lives. To the extent that we surrender to God, we live as redeemed people in this world. However, to the extent that unsanctified areas remain in our lives, we are still living to some extent like unredeemed people. This is exactly why Paul goes to such lengths to point out the normal struggles of the Christian life in Romans seven, and then boldly states:

> *Therefore there is now no condemnation for those who are in Christ Jesus.*
> **Romans 8:1**

Consider my experience, which I regard as a common experience of believers. Early in my Christian life I knew little of love, grace, or kindness. I was often self-absorbed and unmindful of others. I sinned in many ways because of unsurrendered areas of my life. As I grew in the grace of God, He gradually taught me from His Word and challenged me ever more deeply about these things and many others. His lordship increased in my life, and my usefulness to Satan diminished accordingly.

There have certainly been periods in my life in which I was less surrendered to God than I am now. Yet, when I look back at those, I can still recall times when, through whatever amount of surrender I did have, God was still gracious to work through me. God knows that we are unable to repent of sins of which we are unaware. He saved us despite this and gave as spiritual gifts as well. He also knows that it takes time to sanctify us on earth. He is patient with us and gracious to work through us despite our unknown sins.

Satan hates this process and attempts to thwart it by using lies that keep us from taking hold of the grace of God. If he can get us to believe that we are not actually dead to sin, or that confession of generalities will suffice, he will short circuit the plans God has for us. We miss out on the good things God provides for us when we believe falsehoods rather than the Scriptures. However, when the truth of Scripture penetrates us, the lies fall apart, and Satan loses some ability to influence us. The truth sets us free.

Am I saying that Satan is behind all our disobedience? No. Our sin nature alone is enough to make us disobey God. But if we are going to identify Satan's schemes, we had better be prepared to recognize that our tendency to sin is something he will try to exploit. The result of repentance is that we do things God's way more, and Satan's way less. Satan would prefer we never go in that direction because it means fewer sins, less unrighteousness, and less influence in our lives. He is not involved in every choice to sin, but he is likely involved in some of them.

And to be sure, God can get more use out a sharpened tool than a dull one. There is good reason to make effort to sanctify ourselves in Christ. The benefits of righteousness are great, and we are meant to have much to offer to each other and the Church through Christ. My ability to serve Him has only increased as I have learned the things of the Kingdom, and that is what He wants for us.

Satan seeks to derail our spiritual lives to any extent he can by ensnaring us in deceptions that prevent us from living in the fullness of our salvation. To get sidelined by lies is not the work of God, yet each of us can probably see ways in which this has happened to us at various times. Satan uses lies to gain or maintain ground in people, which is why he uses them on the saved and unsaved alike. By understanding Satan's goals from an authority standpoint we can see the bigger picture and be on guard, remembering that the truth of God's Word can set us free from enslaving falsehoods.

Serving the Unsaved

There is another interesting thing about the relationship between believers and the unsaved. Although believers have authority over Satan and demons, and Satan and demons have authority over the unsaved, believers don't have authority over the unsaved. We do not have authority to hold them accountable for their sins as we do those within the church.

We have authority to preach the Word of God to them and to urge them to heed the call of salvation. However, Satan will certainly oppose them responding to the Gospel by using lies against them. A principle focus with regard to the unsaved, then, is to use our authority over Satan's kingdom as servants to the unsaved, so they can be saved. We can portray that like this:

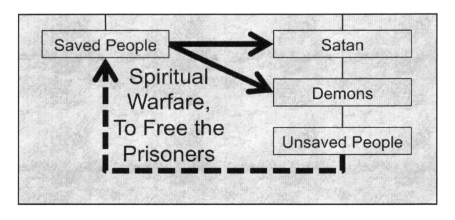

Here, believers are engaging in spiritual warfare[20] against Satan and his demons on behalf of unbelievers, whom they wish to see saved. And that is exactly what Jesus did for us in saving us. He defeated Satan on our behalf so we could be transferred from the kingdom of darkness to the Kingdom of God. Prayer *and* warfare[21] against Satan's kingdom on behalf of the lost should be a normal part of our efforts for them, but in some cases more direct intervention is called for. Mary Magdalene had seven demons cast from her and served the Kingdom of God from then on.

Satan's Influence over People

Satan also opposes believers and the Church, and incites those in his kingdom against all aspects of the Kingdom of God. We see this in many ways. There is opposition from the world to the Bible. The person and work of Jesus are rejected and mocked. The Church is harshly and unjustly criticized. Believers are persecuted and martyred. The list goes on.

But these things do not only happen at a large scale. Individual believers can be targeted by unbelievers, whom Satan prompts against them. I know of a believer who was frequently subject to intense and unjust criticism from a certain person in the course of his work. When he recognized the origin of the criticism as a spiritual attack and began to deal with it from a spiritual warfare standpoint, the criticisms ceased. Some foul spirit was inciting this man against the believer in his work setting, and when the believer dealt with it on the spiritual level, the attacks stopped.

---

[20] It is beyond the scope of this book to explain all the principles and practices of spiritual warfare, but I regard it as an essential activity that believers should be engaged in both for themselves, the lost, and all the other areas encompassed by the Kingdom of God. The reader is urged to learn more from experienced believers, and from the many excellent books on this topic.

[21] I distinguish prayer and warfare for one main reason. In prayer, we ask God to act on our behalf. In spiritual warfare, we act in the authority we are given.

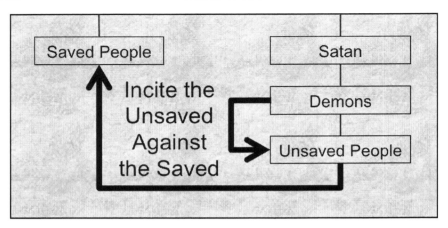

Sadly, Satan is also able to incite one believer against another when he has footholds in a believer's life. This is a source of much savagery and division we see in the Body of Christ, and one of the reasons why prayer and spiritual warfare are required for God's building up of the body in love. The strategic value of unity is so high that it is a primary target at all times. Unity is under constant assault. Consequently, the spiritual and earthly foundations of unity must be routinely and consistently strengthened through prayer and warfare.

Of course it hardly needs mentioning, but Satan even hates those within his own kingdom, presumably because all people are made in God's image. This is a root cause of many wars and atrocities as well as myriads of evil acts that don't seem specifically directed at believers. Satan hates all humans and wants to degrade and destroy them.

Despite all this, Paul is clear that no person is our enemy. He makes this point in Ephesians.

> *For our struggle is not against flesh and blood, but against the rulers, against the powers, against the world forces of wickedness in the heavenly places.*
> **Ephesians 6:12**

When Paul says flesh and blood, he means people. Our battle is not with people. Even if they consider us their enemies, we are not to regard them the same way. Our battle is with Satan and his demons, the rulers, powers and forces of wickedness. When people treat us as enemies, it is commonly because of wicked influences working through them. Our right response is prayer and warfare so as to gain, if possible, rescue for them through Christ. We pray for those that persecute us, but not for their demise. Rather, for their redemption.

Behind the Curtain of Spiritual Warfare

How should we understand the workings of spiritual warfare? As we've seen, angels work mainly behind the scenes and are chiefly reportable to Jesus. In view of this, it seems that when believers use their spiritual authority against Satan and his demons that the heavens hear this and are mobilized to enforce our authority. We know that angels fight against spiritual forces of wickedness. We see that in passages like these.

> *Then he continued, "Do not be afraid, Daniel. Since the first day that you set your mind to gain understanding and to humble yourself before your God, your words were heard, and I have come in response to them. But the prince of the Persian kingdom resisted me twenty-one days. Then Michael, one of the chief princes, came to help me, because I was detained there with the king of Persia.*
> **Daniel 10:12-13**

> *And there was war in heaven. Michael and his angels fought against the dragon, and the dragon and his angels fought back. But he was not strong enough, and they lost their place in heaven.*
> **Revelation 12:7-8**

If angels are the agents of positive change in spiritual warfare, as seems likely, then their involvement probably looks something like this:

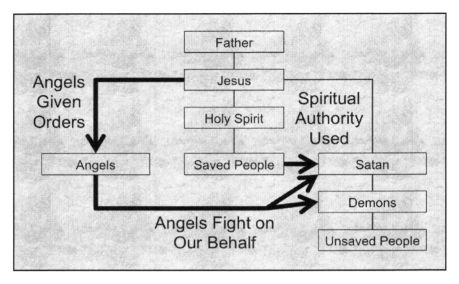

Here, believers are using their spiritual authority (the shortest arrow) against Satan and his demons, and Jesus is sending angels into the battle to enforce this authority by combatting Satan. The activity of the angels is generally concealed from us, with rare exceptions. If we do not see the results we hope for quickly, as is often the case, we should recall Daniel's experience of praying for 21 days *waiting for a message to get through!* Spiritual battles can take time to win.

The Urgency of Spiritual Warfare

This brings us to an interesting contrast. In all the other areas of the Kingdom we have studied, our natural, untrained tendency is always to emphasize action over prayer. We tend to think we can use the Word without prayer, evangelize without prayer, and defeat sin without prayer. We try to live powerful lives through effort without prayer, and we seek for unity without prayer. But the Kingdom Way teaches us that prayer is essential in all these areas. We are to combine faith-based actions *with* faith-filled prayer.

However, when it comes to spiritual warfare, our tendency *is only to pray!* We shy away from direct engagement because it seems frightening, foreign, or weird. We want God to deal with this stuff in answer to our prayers. We want God to bind Satan and put an end to his attacks. We ask God to do these things for us because we don't want to have to deal with this part of the spirit realm directly.

This is the reason that distinguishing spiritual warfare from prayer is so critical. Spiritual warfare *is* faith-based action. It just happens to be the arena of action that we prefer to avoid in favor of prayer. In all the other areas we have studied, our tendency is to take action without prayer; here our tendency is to pray without taking action.

In most things, we tend to believe we have power that we lack, so we pray less than we ought to and gravitate toward action. In spiritual warfare, we tend to avoid using the authority that we actually possess, so we gravitate toward prayer rather than action in the form of spiritual warfare. We recognize there is evil afoot, but we prefer to have God deal with it, rather than take bold action through spiritual warfare and deal with it ourselves. We do this principally out of fear or ignorance.

We like to say "the battle belongs to the Lord," forgetting that the victories in the Old Testament still required the courageous involvement of God's people. Just as then, in the present day Kingdom of God, part of the battle also belongs to us. He has enlisted us to be agents of His authority here on earth.

We flee from the idea of addressing demons directly, but it is precisely here that we are meant to develop boldness. In order to train us toward boldness, Jesus allows us to experience retail assaults from demons in various ways. From this we are meant to gain experience and confidence in the use of authority, and develop the boldness needed to make wholesale assaults on Satan's kingdom. Jesus wants us to be trained to make a real difference in the world around us. Equipping and training us to work through spiritual warfare is part of our development.

Again, in chapters two through six, we saw that action apart from prayer accomplishes little. The need for prayer drives us toward humility and reliance on God. In spiritual warfare, we generally pray, but we fail to accompany that with action by using our authority. The need for action drives us toward boldness and confidence in God.

What is the role of prayer in spiritual warfare? We pray for wisdom, and for God to move into the vacuum left when evil forces are defeated. We pray as a means of abiding in Christ while making war; we pray for others doing warfare; we pray for protection and discernment; we pray for things hidden in darkness to be revealed; we pray for salvation and every other good thing. Prayer is the essential companion to spiritual warfare, but it is not a substitute for it.

Spiritual warfare and prayer are most effective when combined, for example when we call upon God in prayer for wisdom in how we should conduct spiritual warfare, and when we engage in warfare as a means to create openings for God to move in answer to our prayers. It is the harmonious interweaving of these two that is most effective. We use authority to destroy the works of the devil, and we use prayer to bring God's power in *all* the Kingdom areas we have discussed.

Thinking back to our analogy of the sheriff, we can imagine all kinds of situations in which people in a town disobey the law. A sheriff hires deputies, gives them badges, and the full authority of the law. But if they refuse to use that authority, the sheriff's will for the law to be enforced will go unfulfilled, and the deputies will be found negligent.

Picture a man burning garbage in his yard against local ordinances. If a deputy were to drive up and see this, his responsibility would be to intervene to stop the illegal activity, and perhaps issue a citation for the infraction. However, if the deputy rolled up and saw the burning trash and the man, and called his sheriff saying, "Hey, I've got this man burning trash in his yard. Will you come down and arrest him?" The sheriff's response would probably be something like "You're the deputy! You arrest him!"

Imagine if the deputy simply refused to arrest the man and continued asking the sheriff to come and do so, and not only that but called other deputies who all did the same thing, lining the curb, watching the fire and smoke. The sheriff would be angry and remove those deputies from service. The Sheriff's forces should always prevail, but if they disobey him, they yield ground to wrongdoers.

Similarly, believers have rightful authority, but we seldom use it. When we do, it is often fleetingly. Satan is tenacious and doesn't give up ground without a fight. He knows that we can be impatient. Often all he needs to do is fight long enough for us to give up the battle. God wants us to be strong, consistent praying people and bold, determined spiritual warriors that will powerfully use His authority on earth to advance His Kingdom.

However, God will seldom act in situations when He has given us authority, but we don't use it. That is, in essence, what we are doing when we continuously pray for God to stop evil without also using the authority we have been given to oppose the forces of darkness behind the evil. When we pray "God, please bind Satan" we are asking God to do what He has given us the authority *and the responsibility* to do ourselves. Like a sheriff, He generally insists that we do His will. He is not there to do our will in this area.

We effectively disqualify ourselves to a certain extent as long as we refuse to engage in spiritual warfare. The sheriff analogy is fitting. We have been deputized with authority over unclean spirits for our good and for the good of the Church and the lost. Neglect of this area allows Satan to get away with all kinds of things he needn't be permitted to do, and unsaved people perish in their sins because of his unchallenged lordship over them.

Use of spiritual authority is expected of us. It behooves us to use it because it is effective to counter and overcome Satan's work. When we do so, we are reminded of our place with Jesus, we see the truth of Scripture more clearly, and are driven deeper into the Word of God. We also accomplish noteworthy things for the Kingdom of God and obtain testimonies of His intervention. It is part of the abundant and empowered life Jesus means for us to have.

Satan's Bigger Scheme

But Satan has a larger strategy than those we have discussed so far. He opposes every outworking of the Kingdom of God both directly and with specific lies. I've alluded to some of the lies above, but by quickly reviewing all we have studied so far we can identify even more. I've summarized them in the table below. However this list should be considered partial; Satan is crafty and will use any angle to oppose the Kingdom of God. The following are listed in order of the chapters in this book. Consider how common and familiar these are.

Kingdom Principle	Common Opposing Lies
Jesus died and rose again, bringing all believers into union with Him.	• Jesus didn't exist. • Jesus didn't rise from the dead. • We are not joined to Jesus or each other. • Earthly things are more important.
The Word of God is living, active, and more powerful than the words of men. It should be relied upon routinely.	• The words of men are equally potent, or more potent than Scripture. • Scripture is not significantly powerful or authoritative. • Scripture is not relevant today. • Prayer is irrelevant; God will work through our actions without it.
God is both King and Father. The Gospel message includes the call to respond to God as King and Father.	• God is not a king; He will not judge. • God is a harsh king; He will judge cruelly. • God is a bad Father, like your father. • God is a good Father; He primarily wants you to be happy. • The Gospel is unneeded; there is no sin. • Prayer is irrelevant; God will work through our actions without it.
Thorough, specific confession of sins as measured by the Bible is an essential, lifelong discipline for all believers.	• Confession is optional. • Confession of generalities is adequate. • There is no such thing as residual unrighteousness. • There is no link between prior sins and ongoing sins. • You are stuck in your pattern of sin. • Prayer is irrelevant; God will work through our actions without it.
Through abiding, Jesus means to work powerfully in and through us, to overcome sin and minister to others.	• Jesus does not accept us. • You are on your own where trying to be righteous is concerned. • You are on your own where trying to minister effectively is concerned. • Your relationship with Jesus is neither personal nor direct. • Prayer is irrelevant; God will work through our actions without it.

Unity is supernatural, beneficial, and is central to how God portrays Himself to the lost.	• Unity can be achieved on our own. • Unity is too much to ask. • God's plan is the individual, not the Church; why strive for unity? • Prayer is irrelevant; God will work through our actions without it.
Our spiritual environment is complex. Satan has motives and strategies. Believers must use delegated authority to overcome him.	• Satan is not real. • Satan and demons cannot influence believers. • Difficulty in ministry is merely natural; there is no spiritual battle going on. • Spiritual authority is earned, not delegated. • Believers should be afraid of Satan and demons. • Angels should be sought out and exalted. • **No action is needed, just prayer.** (Note the difference here as compared with the lies above.)

We can see from the above that believers and churches today are awash in a sea of lies. Satan is not called the father of lies for nothing. Recognizing this should reinforce how critical both prayer and warfare are to God's work and ours. We can also see how important it is to learn the Scriptural basis for the Kingdom of God, to act on that, and to use Scripture to overcome the lies. We must use the authority we have in Christ to oppose lying spirits and thereby overcome Satan.

But Satan does not only use lies. He will also directly attack believers who are involved in the advancement of the Kingdom. He will use any means he can including other believers that subscribe to his lies, believers and non-believers in whom he has footholds, and governments and institutions of the world. Any of these can be brought to bear against those who would live and minister by the Kingdom.

Consider how the Bible has been removed from schools and the public square in the United States. The Bible used to be taught in schools and read in legislative bodies all over the country. It used to inform the common dialog of the country. Now it is shunned and forbidden to increasing extents. This is the activity of Satan working through governments and deceived people to prevent the Word of God from going into the world and becoming a settled matter. The societal consequences of this have been staggering. It is just one example of Satan opposing the Kingdom of God. I'm sure you can think of other examples for each of the areas we have studied.

The fact is, God has delegated authority to us through Jesus so we will advance His Kingdom in this earthly world. As the Scriptures say:

> *The earth is the Lord's, and all it contains,*
> *The world, and those who dwell in it.*
> **Psalm 24:1**

Rightful authority over all things belongs to Jesus Christ, and He has delegated some of that authority to us. Therefore, let us use the authority He has given us to defeat Satan and free those who are captive to him. Satan will oppose us, so we will need courage, endurance, and persistent dedication to the truth of Scripture to overcome him.

Conclusion

The spiritual environment around us is complex, with numerous possible interactions and several different strategies in use. All believers possess delegated spiritual authority they can use to destroy works of Satan and advance the Kingdom of God. Using that authority in service to others helps create opportunities for God to move with wonderful acts of grace and power. Confident and successful engagement with this environment is an essential skill for Kingdom workers. The authority we have been given is meant to help provide people with evidence that Jesus came from the Father as the Savior of the world, and take away hindrances to them believing the Gospel.

Challenges

If you are unfamiliar with spiritual warfare, begin by reading up on the subject. There are numerous resources in this area. I highly recommend Charles H. Kraft's book *I Give You Authority*. It is an excellent manual on the spiritual authority environment in which we live. It is thoroughly biblical and eminently practical.

Spiritual warfare is best learned from people that do it sensibly. Pray for God to make known to you someone that can train you in spiritual warfare. But be cautious. If the person is immature and does not seem to care about his holiness, he will likely not be well qualified to teach this critical subject. Be sure to be sensitive to God's timing in this. He may have something else to teach you first. The disciples were not casting out demons the day after they met Jesus.

Spiritual warfare will drive you to the Word and enliven your walk with God. It is also something you will get better at. Like any kind of warfare, you will sometimes be caught off guard, sometimes lose or err, but you will also have victories. Be warned that when you begin spiritual warfare, Satan will fight back. Learning to guard your own ground from his attacks while assailing his ground is an important goal. His attacks will grow more subtle over time, so you will frequently be challenged to be on your guard in new ways. This will drive you to Jesus and His Word, and invigorate your life in Him.

Spiritual warfare is meant to embolden us, not cause us fear. If you react with fear to the idea of spiritual warfare, learn Jesus' promises about His presence with us, and observe Him using spiritual warfare to cast out demons and calm storms. The authority you will use in spiritual warfare comes from Jesus, and He is always with you. A confident and capable mentor can also be a big help.

Resist the urge to believe that all sources of trouble are associated with Satan. The world and the flesh are sources of trouble entirely aside from him. To believe Satan is behind every bad thing is to believe a lie from him.

One of Satan's attacks is to tempt us toward unrighteous acts, practices, or beliefs in order to obtain footholds in our lives and undermine our authority against him. One can hardly use spiritual warfare against immorality if one is immoral. Personal holiness strengthens us on the battlefield and makes us more alert to his schemes. In all these things, the Scriptures are your best guide and weapon. They are wholly true, and the truth sets you free.

Overlook

"Your Mom seemed OK," Amy said.

"Yeah, she did. I'm glad to see her getting active and keeping up her friendships and stuff. It was hard for us for a long time to talk about Dad, but now we can."

"I heard you two reminiscing. That's really good. So, where are we going," she asked.

"You'll see. Somewhere my Dad used to take me."

A warm breeze from the open window blew Amy's hair. Joel was driving them up a dirt road through hills on the outskirts of town. The last light of a fiery sunset faded behind them.

"We used to come up here any time of the year, but I liked it best in the summer," Joel said.

"But you're not going to tell me what we're doing?"

"No. You'll know soon enough," Joel answered, grinning at her. "We used to hunt in these hills. I took a big buck when I was in High School, just over that hill there," he said, pointing to the right.

"Yeah, you said you two used to hunt and fish a lot. He taught you all that?" she asked.

"Yeah. He was really good at spotting and tracking, but he said I was a better shot once I got older. He could always find deer. I could never understand how he did it. It was like he could smell them or something. I never knew where they were. He seemed to understand their movements and know where they would be. Used to tell me 'this time of day they'll be doing this or that,' or 'on a day like this they'll be hunkered down and you won't find them out.' Then we'd spot them in the brush along the field line, or something. It made hunting pretty easy. I told him his brain was half deer!"

"Those sound like good times," Amy said.

"They were. I hate that we'll never get to do that again."

"But it doesn't bother you, coming up here?" Amy asked.

"No." Joel paused. "The other day when we were talking, the thing that bothered me the most was that I felt like he let me down about living sensibly. But that doesn't change the fact that the good times were really good. I like seeing this place and coming up here. It makes me sad, partly, but I'm so glad for the memories with him. Seeing this place brings that back for me and I want to enjoy that."

"I think you should. And it sure is a nice night for it," she remarked. She could smell, but not see, wildflowers beside the road from time to time. Nighthawks swirled to and fro in the air above her, barely visible in the deepening dark.

They continued driving a short while more. The stars were coming out in numbers now. In the distance she saw the last line of dusky light on the horizon. Joel was slowing down. As they reached the top of the hills, the car leveled out. He turned toward the edge of the hill, facing west. As he did, the whole city came into view, the river cutting a dark swath through the middle.

"Quite a sight, huh?" Joel asked, smiling over at her.

"That's amazing!" She said, getting out for a better look. The lights of the city came into better view, spreading to her left and right as she walked toward the edge of the hill. A warm breeze blew up the slope.

"This place has been a part of me since I was really little," said Joel, joining her. "We used to come up and watch the boats go up and down the river, and watch trains go through. If there was an eclipse, this is where would come to watch it. He loved this place as much as I do, if not more. Have a seat."

They sat at the edge of the hill, legs outstretched, and watched the lights and the traffic and the boats. Joel pointed out several landmarks she had seen driving through town.

"See how the lights sort of twinkle?" Joel asked.

"It's beautiful. It seems magical, especially with the warm breeze and the stars. I can see why you love it up here. Seems like lots of people would be coming up here. We're lucky to have it to ourselves"

"They do, usually. It's probably just because it's a weeknight that we get it to ourselves.

"My Dad used to say the lights twinkled because of the alternating current going through the city. I know it's not true now. It's just the heat waves in the air. But it made it seem magical, like you say. Like there is a power in the city that brings it to life."

"It's beautiful, there's no question," Amy said.

They sat a while in silence, enjoying the peace and the view. From below a train sounded its horn. They spotted it moving through town.

"It feels so different than Portland," Joel said. "I mean, I know I have more memories here than there, but it still seems like the city itself has a different feel. Like the struggles here are weighing on it. Like it's lost its shine. The economy is down, maybe that's it, but it's like I could tell I was here even if I was blindfolded. Do you know what I mean?"

"Not exactly. Not right now, anyway. Maybe you have to know a place before you can feel that," Amy said.

"Maybe. Maybe you can get tuned into it if you try. This place feels hopeless, like it's lost its horizons. Portland feels, I don't know, proud, driven, maybe even reckless," Joel said.

"That's a pretty good summary of Portland. But I know Portland. I'd have to get to know this place," Amy answered. The breeze blew strands of hair across her face. She pulled them away.

"Mom liked you," Joel said.

"That's good. I like her, too."

"She says you'll be good for me."

"She's right. I will be!"

"You already are."

Chapter 8

The Church in the City

Now after this the Lord appointed seventy others,
and sent them in pairs ahead of Him to every city
and place where He Himself was going to come.
Luke 10:1

In previous chapters, I have begun to allude to the role or place of the Church within cities. In this chapter we will examine the basis for that, see how spiritual authority is delegated to the Church at the city level, and explore what implications that has for us in our mission to bring God's Kingdom to our cities.

The fact that God seems to have a particular interest in cities is easily discerned by studying the words *city* and *cities* throughout the Old and New Testaments. Nonetheless, to call attention to this we will look at several different expressions of this. We're going to say some strong things about the role of the Church in the city, so we want to be convinced that cities have special significance to God.

Jesus and Cities

Jesus had a strong emphasis on cities in His ministry.

> *But He said to them, "I must preach the kingdom of God to the other cities also, for I was sent for this purpose."*
> **Luke 4:43**

> *Soon afterwards, He began going around from one city and village to another, proclaiming and preaching the kingdom of God. The twelve were with Him*
> **Luke 8:1**

When Jesus had finished giving instructions to His twelve disciples, He departed from there to teach and preach in their cities.
Matthew 11:1

When He sent His disciples out to minister, He sent them to cities.

Now after this the Lord appointed seventy others, and sent them in pairs ahead of Him to every city and place where He Himself was going to come.
Luke 10:1

Whatever city you enter and they receive you, eat what is set before you; and heal those in it who are sick, and say to them, 'The kingdom of God has come near to you.' But whatever city you enter and they do not receive you, go out into its streets and say, 'Even the dust of your city which clings to our feet we wipe off in protest against you; yet be sure of this, that the kingdom of God has come near.' I say to you, it will be more tolerable in that day for Sodom than for that city.
Luke 10:8-12

In the passage above, and in the following passages, it is clear Jesus also viewed cities as collectively responsible for their failure to respond to His preaching.

Then He began to denounce the cities in which most of His miracles were done, because they did not repent. "Woe to you, Chorazin! Woe to you, Bethsaida! For if the miracles had occurred in Tyre and Sidon which occurred in you, they would have repented long ago in sackcloth and ashes. Nevertheless I say to you, it will be more tolerable for Tyre and Sidon in the day of judgment than for you. And you, Capernaum, will not be exalted to heaven, will you? You will descend to Hades; for if the miracles had occurred in Sodom which occurred in you, it would have remained to this day. Nevertheless I say to you that it will be more tolerable for the land of Sodom in the day of judgment, than for you."
Matthew 11:20-24

When He approached Jerusalem, He saw the city and wept over it, saying, "If you had known in this day, even you, the things which make for peace! But now they have been hidden from your eyes. For the days will come upon you when your enemies will throw up a barricade against you, and surround you and hem you in on every side, and they will level you to the ground and your children within you, and they will not leave in you one stone upon another, because you did not recognize the time of your visitation."
Luke 19:41-44

The Apostles and Cities

Later, when the disciples began spreading out and preaching the Kingdom of God they, too, paid particular attention to cities.

Philip went down to the city of Samaria and began proclaiming Christ to them…So there was much rejoicing in that city. Now there was a man named Simon, who formerly was practicing magic in the city and astonishing the people of Samaria, claiming to be someone great;
Acts 8:5, 8-9

Peter and John also viewed salvation as having come to the city of Samaria, and went down to minister to the new believers there.

Now when the apostles in Jerusalem heard that Samaria had received the Word of God, they sent them Peter and John, who came down and prayed for them that they might receive the Holy Spirit.
Acts 8:14-15

Later, Philip ministered in other cities as well.

But Philip found himself at Azotus, and as he passed through he kept preaching the Gospel to all the cities until he came to Caesarea.
Acts 8:40

Similarly, Peter's travels in Acts ten and eleven are described in terms of cities. Likewise the first missionary journey of Barnabas and Saul in chapter thirteen notes them traveling through several cities to visit synagogues. Here we find that the response of the people in Pisidian Antioch is noted in terms of the city.

> *The next Sabbath nearly the whole city assembled to hear the word of the Lord.*
> **Acts 13:44**

However, when the people refused to believe, the same judgment prescribed by Jesus was applied to the city as a whole in protest against them, whereupon Barnabas and Paul travelled to yet another city.

> *But the Jews incited the devout women of prominence and the leading men of the city, and instigated a persecution against Paul and Barnabas, and drove them out of their district. But they shook off the dust of their feet in protest against them and went to Iconium.*
> **Acts 13:50-51**

However, when Iconium didn't work out very well, they moved on to other cities.

> *But the people of the city were divided; and some sided with the Jews, and some with the apostles. And when an attempt was made by both the Gentiles and the Jews with their rulers, to mistreat and to stone them, they became aware of it and fled to the cities of Lycaonia, Lystra and Derbe, and the surrounding region; and there they continued to preach the Gospel.*
> **Acts 14:4-7**

Still later, Paul and Barnabas planned a return visit through the cities they had visited before.

> *After some days Paul said to Barnabas, "Let us return and visit the brethren in every city in which we proclaimed the word of the Lord, and see how they are."*
> **Acts 15:36**

And so it goes on and on through Acts. Ministry is to cities, and events are most commonly framed in terms of cities. Philippi is called a leading city. In Athens the city is noted as being full of idols. The Lord tells Paul He has many people in the city of Corinth. Almost everything that happens in Acts is described in terms of cities. It is clear that the focus of the apostles was ministry in the context of cities, for we scarcely see them doing anything else. Even when we do, the cities where various other events take place are usually noted, as with Peter at Lydda and Joppa.

Other References to Cities

We should also note that six books of the New Testament are written to cities.

- Romans
- I and II Corinthians
- Ephesians
- Philippians
- Colossians

The book of Colossians was, in fact, meant for the city of Laodicea as well as Colossae, and there was evidently a letter written to Laodicea that was meant for Colossae, but was lost.

> *When this letter is read among you, have it also read in the church of the Laodiceans; and you, for your part read my letter that is coming from Laodicea.*
> **Colossians 4:16**

Finally, the letters to the seven churches in Revelation are written to, you guessed it, cities. Cities are a persistent theme throughout the New Testament.

The City as a Spiritual Environment

What is it about cities that made them such a focus for Jesus and the Apostles? There are a few things. First, cities tend to influence surrounding areas much more than surrounding areas influence cities. From a strategic standpoint this is important. If the Gospel takes off and revival takes place in a city, people in surrounding areas will be far more open to it than if the reverse happens. When revival comes to small towns, people in the cities typically don't even notice, or can't be bothered to think about it. Cities are key to reaching larger areas with the Gospel.

A second factor is that nations come and go, capturing ground from each other, but cities tend to persist despite this. In most cases they maintain some continuity of identity whether they are ruled by one national government or another. This gives them staying power in times of change. While we in the West haven't personally experienced much of this in the last half-century, it is still a common process in the global milieu. Only in the hands of the most brutal conquerors do we see the cultural identities of cities change significantly or rapidly.

But the third, and most important reason Jesus and the apostles focused on cities, is that cities are spiritual jurisdictions in addition to civil jurisdictions. Jesus and the apostles both pronounced judgments upon cities where their message was rejected. When they encountered this rejection, they shook off the dust of their feet as a protest against those cities. Jesus even pronounced judgments against cities in which He had done miracles, because they did not repent. He compared them negatively to Old Testament cities (Nineveh) that had heeded the messages sent to them, or that seem at first glance to have been worse than them (Sodom and Gomorrah.) The Old Testament prophets also contain many judgments against entire cities.

All this shows that, in God's view, cities are entities in themselves that can be held accountable to obey Him. And if they can be held accountable, then they possess both the authority and responsibility to act collectively on what God declares. These are characteristics of spiritual entities. Cities thus appear in some way to have spiritual jurisdiction over themselves, much as individuals do, and therefore can be held to account to respond to God's Word. When they respond correctly, God brings blessing, staving off calamity and transforming them through the Gospel. When they do not respond correctly, they are held to account, eventually.

Authority in Cities

Recognizing cities as spiritual environments helps us see the following verse as a critical clue to the role of the Church in cities.

> *For this reason I left you in Crete, that you would set in order what remains and appoint elders in every city as I directed you*
> **Titus 1:5**

This verse tells us that God delegates authority to elders *at the city level*, which validates our understanding of the spiritual environment of cities, and brings clearer focus to the roles and responsibilities elders and churches have within their cities.

We looked in depth at authority in the previous chapter. We saw that authority inevitably involves jurisdiction and responsibility. However, the discussion was broad in the sense that we looked only at the authority possessed by all believers. We did not look closely to see if there was anything more specific we could understand about authority amongst believers. But there is more. Elders are designated as those in authority over the church, and we see this sort of biblical structure in place in many churches throughout the world. Elders are given genuine authority as the leaders, shepherds, and overseers of the church. More authority is given to them than to believers generally, and more accountability is expected of them in turn. Adding elders to our organizational chart looks like this:

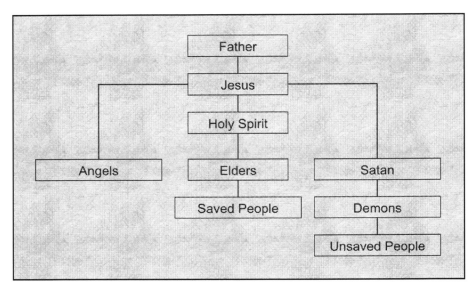

This is in keeping with God's pattern throughout Scripture. God delegates authority constantly and holds those possessing that authority to account for their actions. He delegated authority to Adam and Eve over the earth, and held them to account when they disobeyed. He delegated authority over Israel to Moses and upheld that authority when Korah led a rebellion against him. David understood the authority that God had delegated to Saul, and was unwilling to harm him despite Saul's attacks on him. Paul was respectful to those who held him captive, and wrote at length that believers are to honor earthly authority.

Parents have spiritual authority over their children in addition to their obvious earthly authority. These examples show us that whatever sphere of earthly authority we possess is accompanied by an identical sphere of spiritual authority.[22]

Recognizing that God assigns authority to Elders *at the city level* has tremendous importance for us as we study the Kingdom of God. Many significant implications arise from this. When we realize that the proper jurisdiction of elders, their sphere of authority, responsibility, and accountability, is the city in which they live and minister, we must

---

[22] For more on authority, I highly recommend Charles H. Kraft's book, *I Give You Authority*. These and many other aspects of authority are discussed in great detail.

also think about unity as we studied it in chapter six. Elders are the leaders and overseers of the Church *at the city level*, therefore when God looks for unity in His church, He is primarily looking for it at the city level. Accountability of elders for citywide unity is at the same level as the authority God delegated to them, the city level.

God did not give authority to elders in some general way so they could limit it at their own discretion to the church bodies they serve. Rather, He delegated authority and responsibility to elders at the city level. Tellingly, that is the arena of Christian relationships that is the most challenging and demanding and costly for those in the church to face and navigate well. It is a high responsibility few embrace. The vast majority of churches make little effort to contact or work with other Gospel preaching churches in their cities, or to develop relationships with them. Instead, church leaders often hide behind denominational lines and other artificial divisions, nursing old wounds and their "doctrinal distinctives," rather than acting on the vision of unity we get from carefully studying the Things Above.

But much is at stake in the area of unity at the city level. Because cities are spiritual jurisdictions, our failure to work for unity at the city level amounts to a ceding of spiritual authority to Satan at the city level. As we've mentioned previously, the earth is the Lord's and all it contains, but this is contested ground. Satan fights on here, and God's plan for addressing that is by delegating authority to His church, and more specifically to elders, at the city level. When we neglect or reject unity with believers and church leaders at the city level, we lose our edge against Satan where unity is concerned, *even within our own local bodies*. Why? Because we can hardly abdicate our primary sphere of responsibility (at the city level) and expect to retain much authority at some smaller scale. If we reject unity at the city level we have essentially thrown in the towel and obeyed Satan at the level of our assignment. This automatically creates a foothold for him that he can use to undermine unity in our local bodies.

Consider this map of any city.

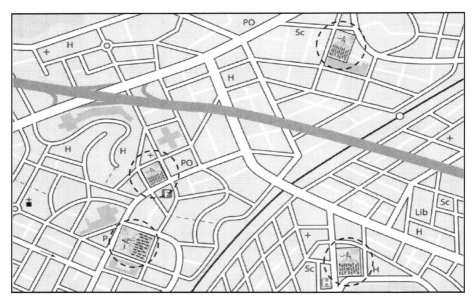

I placed our image of the Things Above at several places within the city. These represent churches with no connections to each other. Their leaders and elders believe they are in God's will. They may even have a pretty good idea about some of the good things God wants for them through His Kingdom. They don't see themselves as having any responsibility toward each other, nor any need for unity with each other. Each church believes they are spiritually self sufficient, that Jesus is their Head, and that they are being obedient to God. They are attempting within their walls to live out the unity of the Kingdom while neglecting or even rejecting unity at the city level. These are the best churches in the city, high performers by all the usual measures.

But this image is pure fiction. It can exist only in the minds of the elders and people of these churches. The believers in these churches are, in fact, actually connected to each other through the Holy Spirit, and the elders of these churches share responsibility for unity at the city level. Furthermore, there is only one Lord Jesus Christ over the church in this city. As much as each of the churches would like to believe that Jesus is entirely Lord in their churches, where unity is concerned, they have not made Him Lord at all. This is true no matter how well they live in accordance with the Kingdom in other ways. They are neglecting a critical aspect of their role and responsibility toward each other and their city. This is the prevalent scenario today in most cities around the world.

But it gets worse. When we abdicate our responsibilities at the city level we lose our spiritual authority over the city as a whole. We are like the sheriff's deputies that keep calling on their sheriff to stop the lawlessness, but refuse to take the actions they are expected to take. We call upon God to save our cities, but reject His means of doing so. We embrace lies from Satan that say we have no need of other churches, no need for unity with our brothers in Christ if they are outside our own walls, and then we expect to defeat Satan in the very city in which we have obeyed him by rejecting unity at the scale God has assigned it. One of the primary criticisms of believers and churches these days is that we fight amongst ourselves. When it is true, it is apparent to unbelievers, and is proof that we have already lost the battle.

Naturally, this makes an ideal point of weakness for Satan to prey upon. He knows that when God's will is done on earth with regard to unity at the city level, he's in big trouble. When churches and church leaders work together in a unified and harmonious way through the Holy Spirit, God blesses that with tremendous outpourings of His power, and Satan loses ground rapidly. His counter strategy against this is to keep us divided and thus ineffective. Revisiting what we've learned about authority, it is easy to see his strategy like this:

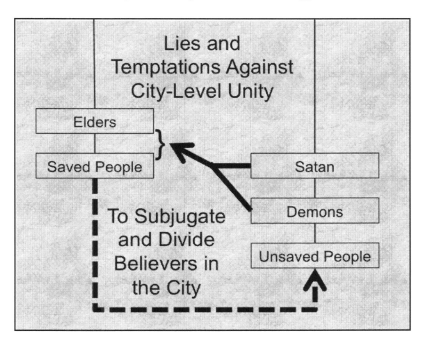

It takes little reflection to see just how successful this strategy is. It is a rare thing for churches and church leaders to work together harmoniously, united in purpose and in the Holy Spirit. So many petty jealousies enter the picture, so many supposed reasons for separation turn pastors and churches against each other, and so many wounds from past divisions go unhealed. Pride, arrogance, and unforgiveness replace love and cooperation. We wind up subject to Satan, forfeiting the victory Jesus means for us to have, the victory He won for us, the victory He offers to us here when we follow the Kingdom Way. Satan often gets his way in cities, but it need not be so.

Citywide Unity in Practice

God has a better way. His way is unity among believers across cities. For His will to be done on earth as in heaven takes concerted, sustained effort to act on the principles of the Kingdom, accompanied by specific and persistent faith-filled prayer. It is rare, but fortunately we have examples of it.

Oliver W. Price[23] recounts in detail the story of Alliance, Nebraska, a drug-ridden city of nine thousand whose pastors, in desperation for their city, set aside their differences and crossed denominational lines to pray together weekly for their city. After only fifteen months, God blessed them and the town. A revival meeting that had originally been scheduled for eight days lasted over nine weeks due to the responsiveness of the people. Nearly ten percent of the town was saved. Marriages and other broken relationships were healed, addictions were overcome, and some that were sick were healed. As Price writes, "Jules Ostrander, pastor of Alliance Baptist Church, said, 'Preparation for this miracle of God was regular fasting, prayer, and cooperation among pastors.'"

Transformative power from God went forth in that city. It is quite possible the pastors did not even know all the reasons that their approach was so successful. One thing is certain, whether they understood the Kingdom principles in detail or not, they had obeyed them. They gathered in unity to be about God's purposes for their city,

---

[23] The Power of Praying Together: Experiencing Christ Actively in Charge, by Oliver W Price.

together. Their obedience looked like the Things Above, and God acted. The results surprised even them.

In 1958, Billy Graham held a crusade in the San Francisco area. He preached for seven weeks. During that time, 28,254 people responded to the message of salvation in Jesus Christ. That was widely publicized at the time. What is not well known is how much prayer was going on behind the scenes. Sherwood Eliot Wirt, who later worked for Billy Graham, wrote about the success in San Francisco in his book, *A Personal Look at Billy Graham.* "Nearly every city in Australia had a Graham prayer group praying for the meetings in California…Soviet Christians in Kiev and Moscow were praying for San Francisco. In India, Germany, and Taiwan it was the same story. Around the shores of San Francisco Bay 1,200 cottage prayer groups gathered weekly, asking God to bless the meetings."

People tend to think that Billy Graham was successful *only* because he was a powerfully gifted evangelist. While there is no question that he was extremely gifted in this way, one of the keys to the success of his evangelistic campaigns was his team's ability to mobilize prayer across cities beforehand. It was a central component of their strategy, and it looks exactly like the Kingdom of God as we're describing it.

Sadly, unity of purpose and mission among churches across cities is typically short lived, and further transformation never occurs. There is a pattern of temporary unity accompanied by limited blessing. When people like Graham come to town, history shows believers will set aside their differences and unite. However, when such people leave, the unity fades and the blessings cease as well.

In contrast, the sustainable model is organic, locally driven unity based on the obedience of local leadership to the mandates of the Kingdom of God. It didn't take Billy Graham to change Alliance, Nebraska. It took Jesus, coming in answer to the pastors' prayers, moving with unexpected power, pouring out blessing and salvation from heaven. That is the power of citywide unity among elders and pastors and churches. When it is sustained over years, the results can be spectacular. George Otis provides numerous examples of citywide transformation in his compelling book, *Informed Intercession.* Consider the following.

Almolonga, Guatemala, a mountain town of nineteen thousand, was known for alcoholism, violence, and worship of local deities called Maximon and Pascual Bailón. The town had four jails that were full to overflowing most of the time. Evangelists were often chased and beaten. Local house churches were stoned. Agricultural production was minimal. Hard times were all around.

Starting in 1974 prayer vigils began. Healings occurred. People turned their lives over to Jesus in droves. By late 1998 the transformation was ongoing and still gaining steam. Twenty-four evangelical churches were active in the city, some with attendance of over one thousand. Nearly ninety percent of the residents identified themselves as believers. The town now operated one jail, barely used. Alcoholism and violence diminished to a trickle. Bars were literally replaced by churches. Agricultural production increased exponentially. The priests of Maximon pulled up stakes and moved to another town. Prayer and fasting for neighboring towns and villages drew twelve to fifteen thousand people.

Hemet, a desert town in southern California, had become a magnet for cults. Scientologists, Mormons, Transcendentalists, and pseudo-Christian cultists had all chosen this city. The town was noted for witchcraft. In addition, neighborhood youth gangs had afflicted the city for decades. Police ferried drugs for dealers and the town was known as a production center for meth.

Pastors began praying together and discovered that the town had long been under the influence of a local spirit whose influence was prevalent throughout the area. As they prayed, God revealed more of the spiritual environment and history of the area, and they began to see breakthroughs. Gang members were miraculously saved. A freak wildfire burned down the Transcendental meditation center, alone of all the buildings in town. The cults shut down. Eventually, with a believing mayor and other city officials, many believing police officers, and a high percentage of believing school teachers, the city bore little resemblance to previous years. Many people came to Christ. The high school dropout rate plummeted, churches now work together harmoniously, and the drug dealers have left town.

Cali, Columbia, once famous as the most corrupt city in the world, had been dominated by the cocaine trade for years. Though home to 1.9

million people, all levels of city government, local business, and banking were beholden to the drug lords. Homicides were frequent, often occurring in broad daylight. Journalists daring enough to report on conditions in the city were targeted in killings. Local pastors were dispirited and isolated.

When pastor Julio Ruibal and his wife Ruth came to the city in 1978, they were dismayed at the spiritual darkness of the city as well as the disunity in the local church scene. "There was no unity between the churches," Ruth noted. Starting there, pastor Ruibal began working to reconcile pastors and improve unity in the church. They began to seek God for increased prayer, unity and holiness among believers. Eventually, a joint worship service was scheduled in the civic center with strained optimism that perhaps a few thousand people might attend. Instead, in an overflowing answer to prayer, twenty five thousand people came, more than half the city's evangelicals. Committed to prayer and praise, many stayed all night. The mayor proclaimed that Cali belonged to Jesus.

In the following months, many believers had visions foretelling the fall of the drug lords, and so it came to pass. Spiritual forces of wickedness behind the drug trade were exposed, all the major drug lords were arrested, and the transformation of the city began in earnest. Ensuing events led additional pastors into bonds of unity with the other churches, prayer vigils continued, and focused attention was devoted to asserting control over the spiritual environment of the city.

The results were astounding. Evangelism took off with greater fervor than ever, the Gospel went forth with power and success, and the name of Jesus was glorified throughout the city. Tremendous church growth kept the pastors overwhelmed, with the numbers coming from new converts rather than other churches. At the heart of it all was communal prayer and cooperation between churches. These events took place over a mere thirty-six months!

What do these stories have in common? The leaders set aside their differences and joined together to take control of the spiritual environment of their cities. Whether they realized it or not, they lived and acted according to the Things Above, and used their legitimate authority at the city level to transform their cities for Christ. God's will was done on earth as in heaven as both the leaders and their people increasingly focused on communal prayer, unity, holiness, and bold spiritual warfare, all of which we see within our study of the Kingdom of God. Most importantly they sustained this approach for years. They were not willing to accept merely a modicum of success when so much power was available from Jesus to do even more.

Praise was also central to the victories in these stories. Just as praise is the feature most common to throne room scenes in the Bible, praise of God and exaltation of Jesus Christ were common to the stories above. Praise characterizes the heavenly environment, and when it flourishes in cities God moves in amazing ways to increase His Lordship on earth. Just as David says…

> *Yet You are Holy,*
> *O You Who are enthroned on the praises of Israel.*
> **Psalm 22:3**

These are the kind of results that come when we persistently obey all that God has for us in His Kingdom. What does it look like from a Kingdom standpoint?

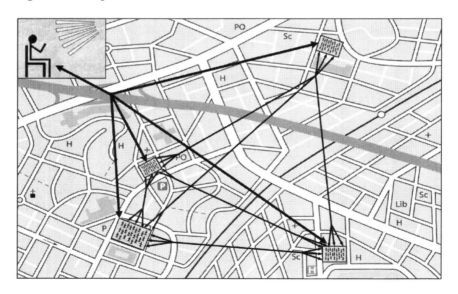

Here, churches are unified, sharing multiple connections with each other. The Holy Spirit is present and working between and amongst them. There is unity at the city level, and Jesus is Lord of all. This is the proper outworking of the Kingdom of God, the means by which God moves with power to transform cities. This is our assignment!

But is this kind of thing biblical? Consider this description of Thessalonica:

> *For our Gospel did not come to you in word only, but also in power and in the Holy Spirit and with full conviction; just as you know what kind of men we proved to be among you for your sake. You also became imitators of us and of the Lord, having received the word in much tribulation with the joy of the Holy Spirit, so that you became an example to all the believers in Macedonia and in Achaia. For the word of the Lord has sounded forth from you, not only in Macedonia and Achaia, but also in every place your faith toward God has gone forth, so that we have no need to say anything.*
> **1 Thessalonians 1:5-8**

This reads much like one of the accounts above. The Gospel rang forth from Thessalonica, just as it rang forth from the other cities we've discussed. God still does this today when we obey all His will for us, including His call for unity at the city level.

Obstacles to Citywide Unity

What are the obstacles that prevent us from seeing the same kinds of results? There are many, but none that can't be overcome with the resources we have in Christ. The largest obstacle is the appalling array of lies we believe about ourselves, our churches, and the city itself. The following is a continuation of the list of lies from the previous chapter. The numbers are the points in the discussion that follows.

Kingdom Principle	Common Opposing Lies
Church unity at the city level is God's design. It is critical to transforming cities. The Church has spiritual jurisdiction over the city.	• Unity within individual churches is possible while neglecting citywide unity, and is enough. (1) • Our doctrinal distinctives outweigh the importance of unity at the city level. Division is justified. (2) • Unity means joining with churches that reject the Kingdom of God as taught in Scripture. (3) • My church can win my city for Christ. (4) • There is no spiritual significance to cities. (5) • Dedication to regional or national efforts and/or dedication to the local body's spiritual health, take precedence over dedication to the city. (6) • Prayer is irrelevant. Only effort is needed. (7) • A little unified prayer once in a while will suffice. (8)

First, unity within individual churches depends on our dedication to unity at the city level, as discussed above. While some progress can be made within individual bodies of believers (churches with a small 'c'), when we neglect unity at the city level, we are willfully ceding ground to Satan at the level of our assignment. In such cases he will always have a foothold within us, and with it, license to undermine unity within our local bodies. We may see some success, but it will be difficult to sustain over long periods.

Second, doctrinal distinctives that divide true believers from each other, or that serve to restrict the field of those whom we'll consider to be true believers more narrowly than the Bible does, pose a danger to citywide unity. The thirty thousand denominations that have arisen since the reformation cannot all be necessary. It is inappropriate to focus on minor doctrinal points that divide us in neglect of the unity Jesus clearly established for us through His finished work. The tendency to do so is born from evil motives. Most of the doctrinal points in dispute between believers and denominations are less well supported in Scripture than the Kingdom of God as we saw it in Chapter One. Indeed, the doctrinal distinctives lie is among the commonest of Satan's ruses, owing partly to the fact that seminary education often focuses far more on intellectual understanding than on obedience to the Scriptures and a coherent understanding of the central aspects of the Kingdom of God.

Third, many people suppose that an emphasis on citywide unity includes a requirement to join with churches and people that clearly reject biblical Christianity and the Kingdom of God. It is not at all necessary to join with such people and churches. In fact, we had better beware to make sure never join with them, for they are in rebellion against God even to this day. Joining with them would only allow Satan to have influence within a work that belongs to God and is His alone.

Fourth, there is also an arrogant assumption among some churches, mainly the larger churches within cities, that they can reach their city on their own, and thus do not need to join with other churches in the work. However, the corollary to the fact that elders across a city share responsibility for the city is that *all the elders and churches* in a city are needed to successfully win the city for Christ.

Similarly, recognizing that God views the Church in terms of cities strongly suggests that when God provides for His Church, He does so at the city level, and not at smaller scales. Consider the meaning of this passage if we view it as God's provision for the Church at the city level.

> *And He gave some as apostles, and some as prophets, and some as evangelists, and some as pastors and teachers, for the equipping of the saints for the work of service, to the building up of the body of Christ; until we all attain to the unity of the faith, and of the knowledge of the Son of God, to a mature man, to the measure of the stature which belongs to the fullness of Christ.*
> **Ephesians 4:11-13**

It is quite likely that God distributes gifts at the city level precisely so that we will have to rely on each other. The idea that God would endow one body of believers in a city with everything needed to win the entire city runs contrary to His desire that we work together to accomplish His purposes. A church that thinks it can reach its city without the other churches in the city is like an amputated limb pretending to be a whole person.

Fifth, Satan loves to convince us that there is no real significance to cities. When he can do this, he has won the entire battle for the city. It is a prime message of his, but it flies in the face of all we see about cities in the Bible, most especially the fact that cities are called out for judgment, and that elders are given delegated authority at the city level. Cities are spiritually significant entities unto themselves, and they are the assigned milieu of ministry that we are to win for Christ.

Sixth, Satan also promotes dedication to supposed prerogatives at both larger and smaller scales than the city as a means to distract us from the city as our assignment. One serious temptation that leads to neglect of the city is an overly large focus on denominational efforts at the regional, state, or national level. Conversely, too narrow a focus on the local body also leads to neglect of the city, and potentially to rejection of other churches within the city. While both of these areas need attention they pose separate and distinct dangers to the Church in a city.

We naturally feel we are contributing to something important by focusing on such things, but when we do so *at any expense* to our express obligations at the city level, Satan gains while our city and the Kingdom of God lose out. Consider these depictions of the amount of effort directed at various arenas of ministry.

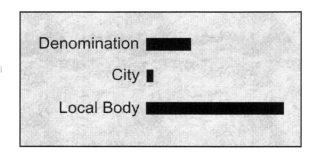

In this case, leadership of a local church is strongly focused on their local body, and the pastor is also highly involved in the denomination or other regional efforts. Unity and the functioning of the body at the city level are sorely neglected. This is a common circumstance. Failure at the city level is virtually guaranteed when the churches in a city behave this way.

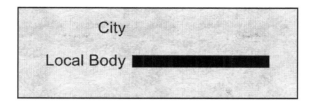

Here is a nondenominational church that is unaffiliated and highly independent of other churches in its city. No matter how good this church seems, it is ignoring critical principles about unity of the Body of Christ in its city. Even at its best, its contribution to the city's spiritual health is likely to be limited.

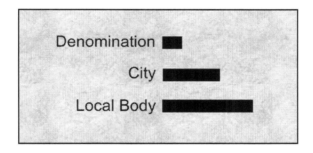

This church is striking a better balance. While there is more emphasis on the local body than on the city, the ratio is such that nobody in the church will be unaware of the church's focus on unity at the city level. They will likely be experiencing guest preachers from other churches, periodic communal worship services involving other churches, and citywide prayer vigils. As a result, personal relationships with believers in other churches will be thriving as well. Denominational involvement should take the form of promoting just this sort of emphasis. All in all, this church looks a lot like one of those in the city of unified churches depicted above.

Churches like this are rare, but they accomplish one additional thing of particular note. They focus their members on something larger than the church they attend. They naturally sustain a missional atmosphere that promotes spiritual health at the city level. The creation of this environment is one of the biggest positive steps a church can take in terms of discipling people.

There is sometimes a place for us to minister at larger scales than the cities in which we live, but in many cases, a strategic retrenchment to the city level is in order. This is not to say we neglect contributions of funds, prayers, and help for those in need elsewhere. Those are certainly modeled in the New Testament. What is not modeled is neglect of our primary assignment in order to do "bigger things" first. Paul and Barnabas both served in larger contexts in their ministries, but this came after years of comparatively anonymous ministry in Antioch.

Few church leaders today have strong credentials where citywide transformation is concerned. Yet many focus large amounts of effort into larger scale, less fruitful efforts. What this diversion of talent and resources is costing us at the city level, God only knows. We would be well warned to consider the principle of faithfulness outlined by Jesus in this verse:

> *And he said to him, 'Well done, good slave, because you have been faithful in a very little thing, you are to be in authority over ten cities.'*
> **Luke 19:17**

Our primary assignment is the city where Jesus has placed us. It is highly probable God will look at our faithfulness in this area when He decides to assign us larger responsibilities, or bless our activities at the local level.

Seventh, we fail when we believe that effort alone, apart from prayer, will suffice to transform our cities. Church unity at the city level is a Kingdom Way core principle, requiring both faith-based effort and faith-filled prayer.

Finally, we kid ourselves if we think a modicum of prayer directed at this goal is adequate to bring the kind of transformation God desires. I discuss this in greater detail in the following section.

Kingdom Prayer and the City

There is a temptation to believe that spectacular results like those discussed above will come quickly and without cost. The key point of the best success stories above (and I urge you to read the original sources) is that devotion to unity, prayer, fasting, and spiritual warfare was maintained over periods of years. Sadly, initial overtures toward unity at the city level are commonly rebuffed. When this occurs, we must persevere with Jesus in prayer. He can break the strongholds in other peoples' hearts, just as He was able to break strongholds in our own hearts when He saved us. But if discouragement is allowed to take hold it will be the end of the story. God honors persistent obedience to our Kingdom calling. Momentary setbacks become His means of training us toward increased prayerful reliance and persistence. We must persevere if we are to win our cities.

Individual and communal prayer is central to our mission as Kingdom workers at the city level, as in all the other areas we have studied. It needs little elaboration by now to see that for God's will to be done in the area of citywide unity, we must obtain His miraculous involvement through prayer. But we also know from our study of authority that legitimate spiritual authority over the city lies in the hands of the elders, church leaders, and the church itself. Submitting to divisions diminishes our ability to use that authority because we've ceded that ground to Satan. However, when we follow the Kingdom Way, we regain that authority and can retake the spiritual environment of our city through use of the authority we possess in Christ.

Part of the job of elders and leaders is, therefore, to lead God's people in spiritual warfare and intercession for the city. We do this recognizing that there will be spiritual strongholds that need to be broken down. Just as Paul says:

> *First of all, then, I urge that entreaties and prayers, petitions and thanksgivings, be made on behalf of all men, for kings and all who are in authority, so that we may lead a tranquil and quiet life in all godliness and dignity.*
> **1 Timothy 2:1-2**

These verses perfectly describe Almolonga and the other cities discussed above. Prayer and spiritual warfare sustained in a context of citywide unity can accomplish such things.

Conclusion

The unity we see among the Things Above is meant to be borne out at the city level. God has given us both the opportunity and responsibility to use our delegated authority to win our cities in spectacular fashion for Christ. True citywide transformation only occurs when elders and leaders take this assignment seriously, overcome the lies that hinder obedience, and persistently work with other churches and leaders in the unity and harmony of the Holy Spirit, all while prayerfully relying on the Lord of the Kingdom, Jesus Christ, to intervene powerfully on behalf of His people. When these conditions are met, God powerfully works to bring astonishing transformation to cities, glorifying His great name in the process. In this way, God's will is done on earth as in heaven, and the world truly sees that Jesus came from the Father.

Challenges

If you are an elder, discuss the biblical role of the church in the city with the other elders and the pastor. Spend time in prayer, fasting, confession, and repentance, then enact a plan to contact pastors of other Bible teaching churches to establish a weekly (or at least monthly, initially) time of prayer. Choose a neutral location rather than any of the churches. Begin praying for unity across the city.

Purposely reconcile with those in other churches with whom you have feuded, or of whom you have been jealous.

Ask pastors, elders and other church leaders in your city how you can pray for them, and if there are any specific ways you can serve them, and follow through. Circulate this prayer list and regularly pray through it publicly.

Pray publicly for the unity of the church across the city. Encourage the people of your church to pray regularly for this. Plan times of confession and repentance for all the people to call upon God for mercy. Confess sins of division and pride that have worked against citywide unity. Encourage people to develop relationships with those at other churches.

Pray for God to show the means toward increasingly unified action. Multi-church worship services, praise events, prayer vigils and the like, are all excellent ways to sustain unity. Participate in work days at other churches and accompany this work with prayer for unity.

Look for ways to increase functional unity in the city as a normal course of weekly activities. Pool youth resources, teachers, childcare, etc., to increase interactions and support for each other.

Be in constant prayer. Instruct all individuals and small groups to pray for citywide unity. Pray at all times for this, never neglecting it. Satan's first line of attack is against unity.

Engage in spiritual warfare for the city, and train others to do so as well. The spiritual environment of the city of yours to take. Satan must be dealt with.

Pray together for the city itself and all the people in it. Pray for the Kingdom in all its present day fullness to come about in the city. Pray for God's Word to go forth and become a settled matter. Pray for people to come to know God as King and Father and receive salvation through Jesus Christ. Pray for believers to develop good disciplines of confession, and that they will abide in Christ and walk in Him. Pray that believers will be unified, and learn to use the authority they have in Christ to thwart Satan's schemes. Pray that sinful institutions and social injustices will be brought to an end. Pray for race relations to improve. Pray for materialism to falter and other idols to fall. Pray for all good things, that God would mightily move and accomplish all His will, transforming the city in His image. Pray that the Body of Christ will truly provide a body *for* Christ, through which He can walk the streets and accomplish all He did while He was here the first time.

Pray that all people in your city will know that Jesus came from the Father as the Savior of the world. After all, that is the whole point.

Conclusion

Can you picture the disciples and the believers of the early church? They turned their world upside down. Something drove them. Something empowered them. Something made them an unstoppable force for God and for good in the world.

They were anchored in God's Word. They used the Word with power because they backed it with prayer. God moved through their use of His Word. Look at them before the Sanhedrin, in the streets and courtyards of Jerusalem, in the cities of Asia and Greece, proclaiming the Word. See how it penetrated their own hearts.

Their God was better than anyone else's. He was the King beyond all kings, a sovereign Lord over all things Who could and would accomplish miracles on behalf of His children. He was clear about His expectations, not capricious. Rather, He was Kingly in all the best senses of that word. He was also compassionate. He understood the frailty of people and was ready to rescue and uphold them through His Fatherly kindness. At cost to Himself, He provided a way for them to become His children, with promises to nurture and build them up through His love and provision.

They were pure in heart, free from unrighteousness. They bore no burdens from past sins. Through confession they kept short accounts with God. Satan had no hold on them because they walked in purity before the Lord. What could hinder them?

They were filled with the Holy Spirit by abiding in Christ. The very power, love and life of Jesus Himself flowed in their veins because they walked in union with Him. As they went they listened to Him, ministered through Him, heard His prayers behind their own, and renewed themselves in Him every day. They died to themselves daily, preferring the life from above, the abundant life of their Savior.

They lived in their cities and towns as one people, rejoicing in each other. United in prayer they pulled down blessings from heaven and drove the Gospel forward from their knees. They were a community of peace, a counter-cultural example to others of what it looks like when God lives among His people.

They shredded the works of Satan because they knew Jesus had trampled him under foot and they had nothing to fear from him ever again. They broke down fortresses of darkness and defeated the spiritual powers of their day.

They seized the spiritual environments of their cities and waged relentless war until entire cities and regions were transformed in the image of God. They did it as one unwavering people, with one clear goal, confident of the authority they possessed to do so.

Nothing else explains the expansion of the early church better than this one fact: They were fueled and empowered by a simple vision that penetrated every area of life and ministry. Their hearts and minds were drenched in a clear vision of the Kingdom of God, and they were backed by His power in carrying out that vision.

We have this vision too. We see all things in our salvation as interrelated in the Kingdom of God. We have all the Things Above: God's Word; a King and Father; our wonderful condition of cleanness in the heavenly court; our intimate spirit-level relationship with Jesus; the pervading unity we share with each other through the Holy Spirit; the authority Jesus shares with us over His defeated foe; and a mission from heaven to make use of all of these to capture our cities for Him.

We have the same opportunity they had. We know the same things they were taught. We see how it all connects. We call on the same God they did to bring the Kingdom from heaven to earth. Nothing holds us back now except the willingness to dig in for the long haul, shoulder to shoulder, and win our cities for Jesus. God still wants the world to know Him as the Savior, and He is always ready to hear and answer our prayers to bring it about when we live by the Kingdom.

Will today's Church take up the full vision of the Kingdom of God? Will our people be drenched in it, and live like it? To the extent that the answer is up to you, will you? It's time we do. Our cities can't wait any longer, and they're ours for the taking!

Afterword

Although many truths from Scripture have been rediscovered in the centuries since the Dark Ages, there is little in this book that could truthfully be called new. The work of Jesus, in which we defined the first of our Things Above, has been studied as soteriology since the time of Christ. The centrality of God's Word has been a core value in protestant circles since the reformation. King and Father are familiar and long standing themes of the Gospel message. Confession has long been promoted as a core discipline of the Christian devotional life. Abiding in Christ, by many names, has its historical and literary origin in the monastics. The importance of unity within the church is at the very least a subject of twentieth century examination. Likewise, spiritual warfare in its modern form traces back to the early twentieth century, and in its earlier forms (exorcism) throughout church history. Citywide concepts of unity and authority appear to be the newest of the major Kingdom themes referred to in this book. Even the practice of relating things on earth to things in heaven has been prevalent in Christian literature for many years.

It is possible that the only new thing in this book is the systematic examination of the Things Above as a source of guidance for Christian living and church practice, and the use of the Lord's Prayer as the key to deriving applications from that study. My desire in writing this book was to develop systematically derived applications that will provide cohesiveness to our teaching and practice, help eliminate gaps in both, and spur believers to unite around a larger vision for ministry than they may have known otherwise. In truth, I have written the book I wish I had thirty years ago, one that would have given me greater focus, and prevented me from wasting as much time as I did.

The Kingdom Way approach is, to my limited knowledge, in its infancy. There remain additional areas worthy of study that were beyond the scope of this book. I urge the reader to consider the ones I have summarized below. I regard these as likely to be fruitful and helpful to the Church. Some of these may prove fruitful enough to warrant books of their own. If you think so, please feel free to write them!

One of these areas concerns worship. In most of the heavenly scenes recorded in the Bible, we see God worshiped in diverse ways. Careful study of these accounts should reveal many modes of worship that could be identified among the Things Above as heavenly worship forms. Which of them do we currently integrate into our personal or communal worship? Which do we lack? Can the worship environment in our churches be expanded to include more of these? What is the role of prayer in our efforts to make worship on earth as heavenly as it can be?

Another area of study should focus on priesthood. Jesus is our High Priest, but we are also called priests. The roles Jesus fulfills as our High Priest in the heavens can be considered Things Above. What are they? Which of these can be understood as proper roles for us? To what extent can we fulfill these roles on earth? Who are the recipients of this ministry? What part must prayer play in our ministry as priests?

Another potentially fruitful area of study would endeavor to map passages of Scripture according to whether they discuss things on earth or Things Above. In my attempts to do so, I have found that certain writers commonly juxtapose discussions of Things Above with things on the earth. The best example of this comes from Hebrews.

> *For you have not come to a mountain that can be touched and to a blazing fire, and to darkness and gloom and whirlwind, and to the blast of a trumpet and the sound of words which sound was such that those who heard begged that no further word be spoken to them. For they could not bear the command, "If even a beast touches the mountain, it will be stoned." And so terrible was the sight, that Moses said, "I am full of fear and trembling." But you have come to Mount Zion and to the city of the living God, the heavenly Jerusalem, and to myriads of angels, to the general assembly and church of the firstborn who are enrolled in heaven, and to God, the Judge of all, and to the spirits of the righteous made perfect, and to Jesus, the*

mediator of a new covenant, and to the sprinkled blood,
which speaks better than the blood of Abel.
Hebrews 12:18-24

The author switches from describing things associated with the Mosaic Covenant straight to Things Above. Identifying these contrasts can help clarify some of the more difficult passages in the Bible, as, for instance, Romans six. Other authors refer obliquely to the Things Above, but seldom specify them. Peter sometimes does this. Having Things Above as a category to use in studying the Scriptures can be helpful.

Another topic in need of further study concerns the many other Things Above that we glimpse in Scripture. Paul commands us to set our minds on the Things Above, which turns out to be a larger task than initially imagined. We've studied several of the Things Above but there appear to be even more. Passages like Hebrews 12:22-24 provide an intriguing glimpse of the heavens. This passage contains some things with which we are familiar as well as additional lesser-known elements that may find support elsewhere in Scripture. What additional Things Above can we identify from passages like this? Which of them find corroboration elsewhere in Scripture? Are there earthly applications that can be derived from any of them using the Kingdom Way approach? In these things we are likely to find ourselves probing the very frontiers of heaven. Caution is warranted lest we find ourselves inventing doctrines and practices that are contrary to other biblical principles, yet there may be fruit to harvest here as well.

Again, Jesus gave authority to His disciples to bless in His name. Paul wrote:

> *Praise be to the God and Father of our Lord Jesus Christ,*
> *who has blessed us in the heavenly realms with every*
> *spiritual blessing in Christ.*
> **Ephesians 1:3**

Aside from the fact that we are directly authorized to bless in Jesus' name, is blessing also a Kingdom Way principle?

Jesus was prophesied to rise with healing in His wings, and Peter tells us that "by His wounds you were healed." Those in restoration and healing ministries pray for healing of the inner and outer man, often calling upon God to bring the wholeness of heaven to people in their care. What other Scriptures support the idea that wholeness proceeds from heaven as one of the Things Above?

Jesus also taught the Kingdom of God both directly and through parables. In the parable of the mustard seed, the Kingdom is compared to this tiny seed, which when planted grows into a large tree, growing far beyond its initial measure as a seed. When the Kingdom of God is acted upon it also ought to grow far beyond expectations. Can His other teachings yield additional insights when viewed in light of the Kingdom as we've come to know it?

Very likely there are additional areas of study as well. My hope is that a precise approach to these will yield additional benefits to us as citizens of the Kingdom of God and help us show the world Jesus as the Savior sent from the Father.

Appendix I: The Kingdom Way Principles

We can organize the ideas in each chapter to provide a more convenient reference. The Kingdom Way defines two areas of focus. The principle that God wants His will to be done on earth as in heaven defines a set of action items for us. The principle that we must call upon God for His will to be done identifies associated prayer concerns we must bring to God to obtain His miraculous involvement.

	On Earth as in Heaven Action Items	**Calling Upon God** Prayer Concerns
Chapter 1: Kingdom Foundation	**Teach the Things Above.** These truths establish key principles on which our lives, churches, and ministries are to be built. It was foundational to the early church. It must be foundational to us.	**We must pray that God will grant us understanding of the Things Above.** Pray that we will set our minds on them, surrendering to them. Pray that God will make them the foundation He means them to be.
Chapter 2: Kingdom and God's Word	**God's Word must go forth and become an increasingly settled matter.** A tithe or more of Scripture should be woven into all of the following… Preaching Correction Teaching Training Exhortation Worship Devotions Prayer Service Evangelism	**Pray that the Spirit of God will go forth with our use of His Word and accomplish all He desires.** Pray that He will make His Word an increasingly settled matter in all areas of life and ministry, and in the hearts of others.

Chapter 3: God of the Gospel	**Portray God as He portrays Himself.** He is a King expecting repentance and obedience from His servants, and a Father giving grace beyond measure to His children through Jesus Christ.	**Pray that God will reveal Himself as King and Father.** Pray that through the Holy Spirit and our use of His Word people will be enabled by Him to respond accordingly with saving faith and repentance.
Chapter 4: Confession and Cleansing	**Develop confession as an essential discipline.** Biblical confession is thorough, specific, and references God's Word. Confession brings cleansing from unrighteousness, which in turn assures of grace and aids in repentance.	**In prayer, confess your sins in a thorough, specific, and biblical way.** Pray for others to confess their sins and for confession to take hold as a discipline in their lives.
Chapter 5: Living in Union with Jesus	**Abide in Christ to live in your union with Him**, so that He can live through you and give you power over sin and the ability to minister to others through His Holy Spirit.	**Pray in expectant surrender to Jesus, inviting Him to live and work within and through you.** Pray for others to learn abiding in Christ.
Chapter 6: Unity in the Church	**Develop church unity through prayerful confession and reconciliation.** Church unity expresses our unity with each other and with Jesus. It is a supernatural phenomenon brought about when God's people collectively abide in Christ. It is to convince the lost of the truth of Jesus.	**Pray for unity from Jesus to underpin all church relationships.** Pray that your unity would become powerful enough to convince the lost about the truth of Jesus.

	Redeem your environment through spiritual warfare. Our spiritual environment is complex. Believers have spiritual authority delegated from Jesus, and are to use that authority for Kingdom purposes. Spiritual warfare is a normal part of Christian living meant for all believers.	Pray for wisdom in your use of spiritual warfare, and to become bolder. Pray for others and your church to use spiritual warfare wisely and courageously. Pray for discernment about your spiritual environment and act on what you learn.
Chapter 7: Kingdom Authority		
Chapter 8: The Church in the City	The elders of the Church in a city must lead the Church toward citywide unity and redemption of the spiritual environment of the city. Elders possess spiritual authority over their city. They also bear responsibility for it. Citywide unity is the primary means God uses to reach cities for Christ.	Pray for citywide unity. Pray for the churches of the city to function as one Church, so Jesus can walk through the city. Pray for elders in the city to lead the Church toward citywide unity and redemption of the spiritual environment of the city.

This table can also be used as a prayer guide. Consider the following prayer as an expansion of Matthew 6:10

Father, we pray that Your Word would go forth within and through us and become an increasingly settled matter. We ask that You would reveal Yourself through your Word as the King and Father that You are, and convince people of their need to reconcile with You through Jesus. We pray that we would grow better at measuring our lives by Your word, and develop good disciplines of confession to receive the cleansing You have for us in heaven. We surrender to You as those dead to sin and alive to You. We welcome You, Jesus, to live Your powerful life in and through us, so that we are transformed in Your image and filled with Your Holy Spirit.

Pour out Your blessing of unity upon us so our lives together prove Your supernatural presence is among us. Train us in boldness to use the authority You've given us to defeat Satan and his forces here on earth. Unify Your people in this city so that we accomplish all your purposes here. Come with power and grace and transform this city, so that all people may be saved, and Your glory be magnified. Exalt Jesus as Your chosen Savior, so the world knows that He came from You.

Appendix II: The Things Above

Below is a partial list of the Things Above with at least one reference for each. It also includes truths derived from the narrative of our journey with Jesus through His death and resurrection.

- You were crucified with Christ - Galatians 2:20
- You died with Christ - Romans 6:8
- You were buried with Christ – Romans 6:4
- You were baptized into Jesus - Romans 6:4 in combination with Luke 12:50
- You have been made alive with Christ – Ephesians 2:5
- You were raised up with Christ – Ephesians 2:6
- You are seated with Christ – Ephesians 2:6
- You are dead to sin – Romans 6:11
- You are in Christ – Ephesians 2:6
- You are alive to God in Christ– Romans 6:11
- Your life is hidden with Christ in God - Colossians 3:3
- You are blameless - Colossians 1:22
- You are holy - Colossians 1:22
- You are complete - Colossians 2:10
- You are united with Jesus - Romans 6:5
- You are united with the Holy Spirit – 1 Corinthians 12:13
- You are united with other believers – Romans 12:5
- You are present in Spirit with other believers - 1 Corinthians 5:3; Colossians 2:5
- You have every blessing in the heavenly places – Ephesians 1:3
- Jesus is wisdom for us – 1 Corinthians 1:30
- Jesus is righteousness for us – 1 Corinthians 1:30
- Jesus is sanctification for us – 1 Corinthians 1:30
- Jesus is redemption for us – 1 Corinthians 1:30
- God's Word is in heaven – Psalm 119:89
- His Word is settled there – Psalm 119:89

- The Lamb's Book of Life is there - Revelation 20:12
- Other books are there - Revelation 20:12
- Jesus intercedes for us - Romans 8:34
- The Holy Spirit intercedes for us - Romans 8:26
- The Father is in heaven – Matthew 6:9
- There is a heavenly kingdom - 2 Timothy 4:18
- God is the King of heaven – Daniel 4:37
- He is glorious - Revelation 15:8
- Jesus is at the right hand of the Father - Acts 2:33
- Jesus is seated at the right hand – Ephesians 1:20
- Jesus has authority over all things and every being – Ephesians 1:21-22
- Jesus is the Head of the Church – Ephesians 1:22
- We share authority in Christ - Ephesians 1:20-22 in combination with Ephesians 2:6
- There is a temple in heaven - Revelation 11:19
- The train of the Lord's robe fills the temple – Isaiah 6:1
- The ark of the covenant is there - Revelation 11:19
- Seraphim are in heaven – Isaiah 6:2
- Cherubim are in heaven - Exodus 25:22 in combination with Hebrews 8:5
- The four living creatures are in heaven - Revelation 5:8
- The twenty four elders are in heaven - Revelation 5:8
- There is a tabernacle in heaven - Hebrews 8:5
- Mount Zion is in heaven - Hebrews 12:22
- The city of the living God, the heavenly Jerusalem, is there - Hebrews 12:22
- Angels are in heaven; there are myriads of them - Mark 13:32; Hebrews 12:22
- The spirits of the righteous made perfect are in heaven - Hebrews 12:23
- The general assembly of the church is there - Hebrews 12:23
- God is a judge - Hebrews 12:23
- Jesus mediates the New Covenant there - Hebrews 12:24
- Jesus's sprinkled blood is there - Hebrews 12:24
- God is acclaimed as Holy - Isaiah 6:3
- Jesus is worshiped with accounts of His deeds – Revelation 4:11
- Jesus is worshiped with singing - Revelation 5:9

- There are golden bowls of incense, which are prayers of the saints - Revelation 5:8
- Those present in heaven fall down and worship on their faces – Revelation 7:11; 19:4
- There is an altar - Revelation 6:9
- The souls of the martyrs are there - Revelation 6:9
- The martyrs can see what is happening on earth - Revelation 6:10
- Those in heaven can speak to God - Revelation 6:10
- People can rest - Revelation 6:11

About the Author

Keith Wood was born in upstate New York and became a Christian believer at the age of eleven, around the time his family moved to Miami, Florida. He attended several colleges and universities, including Moody Bible Institute, ultimately completing a BA in Christian Missions at Montreat College in North Carolina in 1989.

Expecting to go into full time mission work, he was surprised when God redirected him toward a career in Geology. He completed a Master's in Geology at Virginia Tech in 1996 and began work as an exploration and mining geologist soon after. He continues to work in gold exploration for a major mining company in Nevada.

Keith and his wife Patricia have been involved in home- and church-based ministry for twenty years. Keith uses his spiritual gifts of wisdom and teaching to mentor men in his church and community, promote and participate in prayer, and work toward citywide church unity and revival for his city of Elko, Nevada.

The main concepts in the Kingdom Way came as a result of study, prayer, and intercession from 2006 to 2008. Since then Keith has refined the ideas through additional study and application. He began writing the Kingdom Way around 2011.

23312760R00133

Made in the USA
San Bernardino, CA
13 August 2015